D1476172

American Headway

Workbook **3**

THE WORLD'S MOST TRUSTED ENGLISH COURSE

SECOND EDITION

Liz and John Soars

Spotlight on Testing lessons
by Lawrence J. Zwier

OXFORD
UNIVERSITY PRESS

Contents

You will need to listen to the Student Workbook CD / MP3 files online for some exercises. If you do not have the Student Workbook CD or access to the MP3 files online, you can read the Audio Scripts on pp. 84–89.

1 A world of difference

Tenses

1 Recognizing tenses

Read the text. Use the verb forms in *italics* to complete the chart.

Present Simple (x4)
works
Present Continuous (x1)
Past Simple (x3)
Past Continuous (x1)
Present Perfect (x1)
Present Perfect Continuous (x1)
Future forms (x2)
Present Simple passive (x1)
Past Simple passive (x1)

NEW YORK CITY – AMERICA'S MELTING POT

There are over three million immigrants living in New York City today. Why do they come to the Big Apple?

RYUU TAKAHASHI, 30, from Japan, *works* in the city. He says, "I *love* living in New York. It's dynamic and extremely international. People *come* here to find work but then realize that it's really exciting. My company *is owned* by a Japanese bank, and I*'m going out* with an American woman. I*'ll stay* here for another five or six years."

LUISA JARAMILLO, 21, from Colombia, *came* to New York City three years ago to learn English and *has been* here ever since. "I *met* my boyfriend while I *was working* at the Plaza Hotel. I *was employed* in Accounts. I now think of New York City as my home. We*'re going to get* married next year."

CÉLINE ABADIE, 28, from France, *found* a job in two weeks. "Unemployment is high in France, especially for young people. I *know* friends in Paris who *have been looking* for work for six months," she said. "There is a sense of opportunity here in New York. Anything is possible."

2 Producing tenses

Complete the sentences using the verb in the box and the tense given.

make

1. PRESENT SIMPLE
   I work for a company that ___makes___ printers.

2. PRESENT SIMPLE PASSIVE
   The printers _____ in China.

3. PRESENT PERFECT
   We _____ a big profit this year.

take

4. PAST SIMPLE
   I _____ my daughter to the zoo yesterday.

5. *GOING TO* FUTURE
   I _____ her to the movies tonight.

6. PAST SIMPLE PASSIVE
   This photo of her _____ on vacation last year.

be

7. PRESENT PERFECT
   I _____ to every country in Asia on business.

8. PAST SIMPLE
   This time last year I _____ in Thailand.

9. *WILL* FUTURE
   Next week I _____ in Mexico.

work

10. PRESENT CONTINUOUS
    I _____ at home this week.

11. PAST CONTINUOUS
    I _____ in Boston the week before last.

12. PRESENT PERFECT CONTINUOUS
    I'm tired. I _____ hard recently.

3 Tenses and time expressions

Put the verb in the correct tense for the time expressions.

1. He usually __goes__ (go) jogging ...
   - every day.
   - twice a week.
   - on Friday mornings.

2. I _____ (go) to Florida
   - last year.
   - in 2004.
   - six months ago.

3. We _____ (live) here ...
   - for five years.
   - since July.
   - all our lives.

4. What _____ you _____ (do) ...
   - right now?
   - these days?
   - this week?

5. I _____ (see) you ...
   - next week.
   - later.
   - tonight.

Auxiliary verbs

4 Auxiliary verb or full verb?

Is the verb in **bold** used as an **auxiliary** verb (**A**) or a **full** verb (**F**)?

1. **A** **Have** you ever been to China?
   F They **have** three children.

2. ☐ I **do** my homework every night.
   ☐ Where **do** you come from?

3. ☐ They **are** nice children.
   ☐ They **are** learning English.

4. ☐ What time **did** you get home?
   ☐ We **did** a play at school today.

5. ☐ Brazil **has** won the World Cup five times.
   ☐ Brazil **has** some beautiful beaches.

6. ☐ I **was** having dinner at 8:00.
   ☐ I **was** at home.

7. ☐ My sister **does** yoga every week.
   ☐ What **does** your father do?

8. ☐ My son **is** at school.
   ☐ He **is** taught Spanish by my old teacher.

5 Asking questions

1 Read the *Amazing facts*. Some information is missing. Write questions to get the information.

Amazing facts

1. The human heart beats _____ times a year.

2. The solar system was formed _____ years ago.

3. _____ people are born every day.

4. Oil was first discovered in Saudi Arabia in _____ .

5. The U.S. spends _____ on defense every year.

6. Right now, the International Space Station is flying at _____ .

7. Shakespeare had _____ children.

8. _____ people were killed in the Second World War.

9. The U.S. President earns _____ a year.

10. The average marriage in the U.S. lasts _____ years.

1. How many <u>times does the human heart beat a year</u> ?
2. How long ago _____ ?
3. How many _____ ?
4. When _____ ?
5. How much _____ ?
6. How fast _____ ?
7. How many _____ ?
8. How many _____ ?
9. How much _____ ?
10. How long _____ ?

2 **CD1** **2** Listen, check, and complete the text with the answers you hear.

6 Replying with questions

Reply to these statements with a question.

1. Joan's writing an e-mail.
   Who's <u>she writing to</u> ?

2. David speaks four languages.
   Which _____ ?

3. I got some great presents for my birthday.
   What _____ ?

4. Joy and Eric paid a lot of money for their house.
   How much _____ ?

5. I'm going to the movies tonight.
   What _____ ?

6. We had a wonderful vacation.
   Where _____ ?

7. Bye! See you later!
   Where _____ ?

8. Jamal's talking on the phone.
   Who _____ ?

7 Negatives

Everything that **A** says is wrong! Complete **B**'s lines as she corrects him.

1. **A** Jane and Ann live in the center of town.
   B <u>They don't live in the center</u> . They live in the suburbs!

2. **A** They had a great vacation.
   B _____ . It rained every day!

3. **A** Jane works in an office.
   B _____ . She's a teacher!

4. **A** Ann has a brother.
   B _____ . She's an only child!

5. **A** They've shared an apartment for years.
   B _____ . They only met last August!

6. **A** They have a lot of friends.
   B _____ . They don't know anybody!

7. **A** Jane went to college.
   B _____ . She left school at 16!

8. **A** Ann has to work at night.
   B _____ . She's a librarian!

8 Short answers

Read the conversation. Complete the sentences with short answers.

S Hi, Amy. I haven't seen you for ages. Have you been away?

A (1) Yes, _I have_ . I've been in Australia for six months.

S Wow! Did you have a good time?

A (2) Yes, _____ . It was amazing.

S Were you traveling around?

A (3) No, _____ . When I first got there, I stayed in Sydney for three months.

S Don't your aunt and uncle live there?

A (4) Yes, _____ . I stayed with them for a few weeks, then I got a place of my own with friends.

S Did you rent an apartment?

A (5) No, we _____ . We rented a house near the beach. Then we went up the east coast.

S And what did you think of Australians? They're really nice, aren't they?

A (6) Yes, _____ . Very easy going.

S Don't they spend a lot of time outdoors in the sunshine?

A (7) Yes, _____ . But the sun doesn't shine all the time. On the way back I went to Thailand. Have you been there?

S (8) No, _____ . But I'd love to. What are you doing now? Are you looking for a job?

A (9) Yes, _____ . But it isn't easy. Do you have any ideas where I could look?

S (10) No, _____ . Sorry. But I'm sure you'll manage. Anyway, Amy, it's good to see you again.

A Thanks. And you. I'll see you around. Bye!

CD1 3 Listen and check.

Pronunciation

9 Phonetic symbols – vowel sounds

1 Look at the symbols for vowel sounds.

Short vowel sounds					
/ɪ/	/ɛ/	/æ/	/ɔ/	/ʊ/	/ʌ/
big	pen	cat	dog	put	sun
_____	_____	_____	_____	_____	_____
_____	_____	_____	_____	_____	_____

Long vowel sounds				
/i/	/ɑr/	/ɔr/	/u/	/ər/
see	car	more	two	bird
_____	_____	_____	_____	_____
_____	_____	_____	_____	_____

CD1 4 Listen and repeat.

2 Write these words under the correct symbol in the chart in Exercise 1.

push	heart	red	cool	saw	eat
ran	war	hit	first	bus	build
friend	group	foot	black	wash	does
meet	start	short	work		

CD1 5 Listen, check, and repeat.

▶▶ **Phonetic symbols p. 93**

10 Word stress

CD1 6 Listen and put the words in the correct column according to the stress pattern.

typical	education	foreign	immediate
ambitious	regret	Internet	economic
sunshine	reception	correct	community

1. ●● country _____ _____

2. ●● polite _____ _____

3. ●●● important _____ _____

4. ●●● grandfather _____ _____

5. ●●●● population _____ _____

6. ●●●● experience _____ _____

Vocabulary

11 Grammar words

Match words in **A** with a grammar term in **B**.

A		B
1.	[f] write, want	a. preposition (prep)
2.	[ ] she, him	b. adjective (adj)
3.	[ ] car, tree	c. adverb (adv)
4.	[ ] can, must	d. modal auxiliary verb
5.	[ ] slowly, always	e. pronoun (pron)
6.	[ ] nice, pretty	f. full verb
7.	[ ] bigger, older	g. count noun (C)
8.	[ ] to like	h. noncount noun (U)
9.	[ ] a	i. comparative adjective
10.	[ ] on, at, under	j. superlative adjective
11.	[ ] hoping, living	k. infinitive with *to* (infin with *to*)
12.	[ ] the	l. *-ing* form of the verb (*-ing* form)
13.	[ ] fastest, hottest	m. past participle (pp)
14.	[ ] done, broken	n. definite article
15.	[ ] rice, weather	o. indefinite article

12 Word formation

Complete the sentences using the word in CAPITALS in the correct form.

1. My brother is a __musician__ . MUSIC

2. A trumpet is a _____ instrument. MUSIC

3. I drive a very _____ car. ECONOMY

4. I spend more than I earn. I must _____ . ECONOMY

5. _____ give governments advice about finance. ECONOMY

6. _____ have a lot of responsibility for their staff. EMPLOY

7. The _____ rate in the U.S. is about 9%. EMPLOY

8. I'm self-_____ . I don't work for anyone else. EMPLOY

13 Words that go together

Match a word in **A** with a line in **B**.

A		B
1.	[b] go on	a. a business
2.	[ ] make	b. the Internet
3.	[ ] win	c. a photograph
4.	[ ] start	d. home
5.	[ ] take	e. archaeology
6.	[ ] do	f. a prize
7.	[ ] study	g. an appointment
8.	[ ] leave	h. your best

14 Different meanings

Look at the dictionary entry for the word *course*.

course /kɔrs/ noun
1 [C] a course (in/on sth) a complete series of *lessons: I've enrolled in an English course. ▪ A course in self-defense.* **2** [C] one of the parts of a meal: *a three-course lunch ▪ I had chicken for the main course.* **3** [C] an area where golf is played or where certain types of race take place: *a golf course ▪ a racecourse* **4** [C] a course (of sth) a series of medical treatments: *The doctor put her on a course of radiation therapy.* **5** [C, U] the route or direction that sth, especially an airplane, ship, or river takes: *We changed course and sailed toward land.*

Match the word *course* in the sentences with a meaning 1–5 in the dictionary entry.

a. I'm on a *course* of antibiotics. ___

b. My daughter did a *course* in interior design. ___

c. We had to run a five-mile cross-country *course*. ___

d. A three-*course* meal consists of a starter, a main course, and a dessert. ___

e. The road follows the *course* of the river. ___

Prepositions

15 Verb + preposition

1 Complete the sentences with a preposition from the box.

| of | about | to | at | with | for | as | on |

1. I think you're wrong. I don't agree _____ you at all.
2. You look worried. What are you thinking _____ ?
3. Look _____ that picture. Isn't it beautiful!
4. Are you listening _____ me?
5. If you have a problem, talk _____ the teacher.
6. **A** What were you and Alex talking _____ ?
   B Oh, this and that.
7. We might have a picnic tomorrow. It depends _____ the weather.
8. **A** What do you think _____ Pete?
   B I really like him.
9. Where's the cash register? I need to pay _____ this book.
10. **A** I lost your pen. Sorry.
    B It's all right. Don't worry _____ it.
11. **A** What are you looking _____ ?
    B My coat. Have you seen it?
12. Henry works _____ a taxi driver.

Listening

16 The world of work

1 **CD1 7** Listen to an interview about Polish people (Poles) living in Britain. In which order (1–6) do you hear about the following?

- [ ] why Poles come to Britain
- [ ] how people in Britain regard these new immigrants
- [ ] permits and documentation needed in Britain
- [ ] the Polish population now living in the UK
- [ ] how easily Poles settle in Britain
- [ ] the first large group of Polish immigrants to the UK

2 Now answer these questions.

1. What is different about the most recent wave of immigrants to Britain?
2. What happened in 2004?
3. Why can Poles find jobs with British companies before they come to Britain?
4. Why are British employers keen to employ Polish workers?
5. Why don't people from the older Polish community always welcome the new arrivals?

3 Complete the extracts from the interview with the correct form of the verbs in parentheses.

1. Now, you _____ (probably hear) that the Polish community in Britain _____ (grow) faster than any other at the moment, but _____ (you know) that the total number of Poles living in Britain _____ (now estimate) to be three quarters of a million?

2. So are these all Poles who _____ (arrive) in the UK recently?

No, they aren't. Many of them _____ (live) here for a long time. About 200,000 Poles _____ (settle) in Britain after 1945, and about 150,000 of those _____ (still live) here in the early 1990s.

3. Yes, since the European Union _____ (expand) in 2004, Polish people _____ (take advantage) of the opportunity to relocate here without restrictions.

CD1 7 Listen again and check.

Grammar: Present Simple and Continuous – active and passive
Vocabulary: Adjectives that describe character • Phrasal verb + noun
Pronunciation: -*s* at the end of a word • States and activities

Present tenses

1 Recognizing tenses

Read the text. Use the present verb forms in *italics* to complete the chart.

Present Simple (x 7)
lives

Present Continuous (x 6)

Present Simple passive (x 2)

Present Continuous passive (x 1)

AMERICAN ARTIST, BORN AND BRED

ANNIE McLEAN is one of the U.S.'s best living artists. HENRY LUCAS went to visit her at her home.

Annie McLean was born in Boston, Massachusetts. She studied at the Rhode Island School of Design, in Providence. She *lives* in a small New England coastal town with her husband, Duncan, and her three children. Home is a 200-year-old farmhouse which *overlooks* the sea. Duncan is a writer and *is working* on his new book.

Annie *paints* animals and wildlife. "I *paint* what I *see* around me," she told me, "birds, animals, trees, and flowers. I *find* my work totally absorbing. I *work* outside in the open air for as long as it is light, from dawn until dusk—about 13 hours a day in summer, though less now because it's winter."

Her work *is becoming* increasingly popular, and she *is planning* to open a gallery in her town. "Right now I'*m painting* a series of wild flowers," she said to me over coffee in her studio.

The town *is inhabited* by 700 people who *are employed* mainly in the fishing industry. The population *is falling* because young people *are leaving* the town to look for work. The town *is being developed* as a tourist destination—50,000 visitors come every year—but it is big enough for Annie to escape and find her inspiration. ∿

2 Producing tenses

Complete the sentences using the verb in the box and the tense given.

paint

1. PRESENT SIMPLE
Annie __paints__ animals and wildlife.

2. PRESENT CONTINUOUS
Right now she _____ a series of wild flowers.

find

3. PRESENT SIMPLE
She _____ her work totally absorbing.

4. PRESENT SIMPLE PASSIVE
A lot of rare birds _____ near her home.

think

5. PRESENT CONTINUOUS
Annie _____ of opening a small gallery.

6. PRESENT SIMPLE PASSIVE
She _____ to be one of the U.S.'s most important artists.

know

7. PRESENT SIMPLE PASSIVE
Her work _____ all over the world.

8. PRESENT SIMPLE
She _____ most of the people in her town.

work

9. PRESENT SIMPLE
She _____ in the open air from dawn until dusk.

10. PRESENT CONTINUOUS
She _____ only _____ six hours today because it's winter.

3 Questions

Here are some answers to questions about Annie McLean. Write the questions.

1. Where _does she live_ ?
In a small New England coastal town.

2. How many _____ ?
Three.

3. What _____ ?
He's a writer.

4. _____ ?
Animals and wildlife.

5. Where _____ ?
In the open air.

6. _____ doing right now?
She's painting a series of wild flowers.

7. _____ young people _____ ?
Because there aren't any jobs.

8. _____ ?
50,000.

4 Negatives

Correct the information in these sentences.

1. Annie lives in Canada.
She doesn't live in Canada. She lives in the U.S.

2. Her husband is a farmer.

_____

3. Annie paints portraits.

_____

4. She's painting a series of wild birds.

_____

5. The people in the town are employed in farming.

_____

6. Young people are leaving the town to get married.

_____

Adverbs

5 Adverbs of time and frequency

Put the adverbs in parentheses in the correct place in the sentence. Some may go in more than one place.

1. I drink coffee.
   (never / in the evenings)

   I never drink coffee in the evenings.

2. How do you see Julie?
   (often / these days)

   _____

3. I go to the movies.
   (hardly ever / anymore)

   _____

4. I bump into my old girlfriend.
   (from time to time)

   _____

5. Do you come here?
   (often)

   _____

6. I don't cook. I eat out.
   (much / usually)

   _____

7. I see my grandparents.
   (only / once a month)

   _____

8. I wash my hair, and I have it cut.
   (twice a week / every month)

   _____

9. Children play on their own outdoors.
   (rarely / nowadays)

   _____

10. I spend commuting.
    (three hours a day / sometimes)

    _____

Pronunciation

6 -s at the end of a word

The pronunciation of -s at the end of a word can be /s/, /z/, or /ɪz/.

1. /s/   In these words, the final -s is pronounced /s/.

   CD1 8 Listen and repeat.

pots	hits	parents	laughs	likes
stops	chefs	hates	months	wants

2. /z/   In these words, the final -s is pronounced /z/.

   CD1 9 Listen and repeat.

friends	comes	has	eggs	goes
news	gives	does	sees	clothes
lessons	sings	travels	pens	moves

3. /ɪz/   In these words, the final -s is pronounced /ɪz/.

   CD1 10 Listen and repeat.

nurses	washes	raises	watches
brushes	misses	switches	buses
challenges	places	wages	revises

4. Put these words into the correct column.

changes	surfs	bats	sells	buildings
loves	beaches	weeks	organizes	learns
sentences	wants	breathes	cooks	matches

/s/	/z/	/ɪz/
groups	jobs	lunches
_____	_____	_____
_____	_____	_____
_____	_____	_____
_____	_____	_____

   CD1 11 Listen, check, and repeat.

   ▶▶ **Phonetic symbols p. 93**

Present Simple and Continuous

7 Questions and negatives

Read the text and do the exercises.

Complete the questions in the Present Simple.

1. How fast _____?
   300 km/h (190 mph).

2. How many passengers _____?
   800.

3. How long _____?
   Two hours 48 minutes.

4. How much _____?
   125,000 yen ($1,250).

5. How many women _____?
   1,300.

Complete Kumiko Mogi's questions in the Present Continuous.

6. What _____?

7. Who _____?

8. How many bags _____?

9. What books or newspapers _____?

Write the negative sentences.

10. Mogi / not sell / ice cream / winter.

   _____

11. People / not want beef or rice / breakfast.

   _____

12. She / not have lemonade.

   _____

13. The trolley girls / not sit down.

   _____

14. Mogi / not turn / back towards / customers.

   _____

15. She / not want / do a different job.

   _____

THE QUEEN OF FAST FOOD ON JAPANESE TRAINS

KUMIKO MOGI is, at 27, far and away the most successful snack saleswoman on the Japanese train network. Bullet trains travel at ▧ km/h and carry ▧ passengers, but they have no dining cars. Mogi works on the train that goes from Yamagata to Tokyo. The journey takes ▧ . Ordinary wagon girls average about 25,000 yen ($250) on the six-hour return trip. Mogi earns ▧ .

She is more successful than all her colleagues, and she is now an instructor to the ▧ women who work on the East Japan Railways bullet trains.

"The important thing in this job," she says, "is to know the customers. I size them up very carefully as they are getting on the train, and I ask myself these questions.

- *What / the passengers / wear?*
- *Who / they / travel / with?*
- *How many bags / they / carry?*
- *What books or newspapers / they / read?*"

Based on the answers, she decides what people will want to eat and drink. "If it's hot, I sell a lot of banana cakes and iced coffee for breakfast. No ice cream in winter. People buy lunchboxes of beef and rice. I also have dried fish, salted beef tongue, and juice. But no lemonade."

No seats are provided for the trolley girls. They carry on selling until the door opens at the terminal.

Unlike her competition, Mogi pulls her trolley, she doesn't push it. "I never turn my back towards the customers. I can look at their faces all the time and work out what they want."

Does she want to get a promotion and do something different? "Of course not," she replies. "You can see that I'm perfect for this job."

States and activities

8 Present Simple or Continuous?

Remember the verbs that rarely take the continuous.

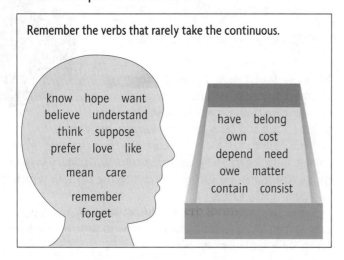

know   hope   want
believe   understand
think   suppose
prefer   love   like

mean   care

remember
forget

have   belong
own   cost
depend   need
owe   matter
contain   consist

1 Complete the sentences with one of the verbs from the box.

have	consist	depend	~~belong~~	prefer
not matter	need	cost	smell	owe
hope	look	own	remember	not suit

1. This book __belongs__ to me.
2. The U.S. _____ a population of 306 million.
3. Water _____ of hydrogen and oxygen.
4. "I forgot your book again. Sorry."
   "It _____ . You can bring it later."
5. I _____ a haircut. My hair is too long.
6. _____ you _____ this apartment, or do you rent it?
7. Gasoline _____ about $2.50 a gallon.
8. I've borrowed so much money. How much do I _____ you?
9. You _____ pretty. Where did you get that dress?
10. Congratulations on your wedding. I _____ you'll be very happy.
11. The sweater fits you very well, but the color _____ you.
12. We might have a picnic. It _____ on the weather.
13. I like both tea and coffee, but I _____ tea.
14. You _____ nice. What perfume are you wearing?
15. I _____ when you were a little girl. You were very cute.

2 Complete the pairs of sentences. Use the verb in **bold** once in the Present Simple and once in the Present Continuous.

1. **come**

   Julian _____ from Peru.

   We _____ on the ten o'clock train.

2. **not have**

   He _____ any children.

   He _____ breakfast this morning.

3. **see**

   I _____ the dentist next week. I think I need a filling.

   I _____ what you mean, but I don't agree.

4. **not think**

   I have an exam tomorrow, but I _____ about it.

   I _____ she's very clever.

5. **watch**

   Be quiet. I _____ my favorite TV show.

   I always _____ it on Thursday evenings.

6. **not enjoy**

   We _____ this party at all. The music is too loud.

   We _____ big parties.

7. **use**

   This room _____ usually _____ for big meetings.

   But today it _____ for a party.

Present passive

9 Recognizing tenses

Read the text. Find examples of the Present Simple and Present Continuous, active and passive, and complete the chart.

Present Simple active (x 3)
Present Continuous active (x 3)
Present Simple passive (x 6)
is based
Present Continuous passive (x 1)

10 Office life

Put the verbs in parentheses in the Present Simple passive.

1. In 70% of offices, employees _____ (ban) from using social networking sites such as Facebook.

2. 40% of Internet use in the office _____ (not relate) to work.

3. Work hours _____ often _____ (use) to conduct personal business.

4. 45% of work time _____ (waste) on chat, drinking coffee, and taking personal phone calls.

5. Open-plan offices _____ (dislike) by 40 % of workers.

6. Team-bonding days _____ (despise) by nearly everyone.

7. Most employees complain that they _____ (overwork) and _____ (not appreciate).

8. Many people _____ (stress) by the number of e-mails they receive.

9. More than six trillion business e-mails _____ (send) worldwide every year.

10. Stress at work _____ (associate) with the risk of heart disease. It _____ (also know) to cause depression.

THE U.S. ECONOMY

■ The U.S. economy *is based* on the goods and services industries—insurance, banking, tourism, government, and retail. With globalization and the communications revolution, goods, services, and finance *move* freely and easily around the world, and this *is playing* a big part in changing the U.S.

■ The U.S. *exports* industrial supplies, motor vehicle parts, food, and beverages. It *imports* raw materials, cars, gas, and oil. Most of its electrical and electronic goods *are imported* from China, Canada, and Mexico. Only 17% of the working population *is employed* in manufacturing. 83% is employed in service-producing industries.

■ Many businesses in the public service sectors such as water, electricity and gas, railways, and airports, *are owned* privately.

■ Americans *are being taxed* at a local, state, and federal level. The proportion of time that Americans spend working *is falling*. Young people *are staying* longer in education. More women *are employed* than men. 7.5% of women *are unemployed*, compared to 9.8% of men.

Vocabulary

11 Adjectives that describe character

1 Match a description in **A** with an adjective in **B**.

A		B
1. **g** She likes being with people and is fun.		a. generous
2. ☐ She always has to get everything she wants.		b. optimistic
3. ☐ He always gives great presents.		c. kind
4. ☐ She cares about people and wants to make them happy.		d. shy
5. ☐ She wants to do really well in life.		e. eccentric
6. ☐ He only ever thinks of himself.		f. rude
7. ☐ She always looks on the bright side of things.		g̶. sociable
8. ☐ He hates meeting people and having to talk to them.		h. spoiled
9. ☐ She has some very strange ideas.		i. ambitious
10. ☐ He never does any work at all.		j. lazy
11. ☐ You never know how he's going to be, happy or sad.		k. moody
12. ☐ He always says things to upset and annoy people.		l. selfish

2 Match these adjectives with their opposites in Exercise 1.

1. **a** cheap
2. ☐ hardworking
3. ☐ unselfish
4. ☐ cheerful
5. ☐ confident
6. ☐ antisocial
7. ☐ polite
8. ☐ unkind
9. ☐ pessimistic
10. ☐ unambitious

3 Complete the sentences with an adjective from Exercise 2.

1. The Japanese have a reputation for being ___**polite**___ .
2. He's so _____—he never buys anyone a drink.
3. I'm afraid I'm pretty _____—I hate going to parties and making small talk.
4. She always thinks the worst is going to happen. She's very _____ .
5. He's so _____ . He's always the first to arrive in the office and the last to leave.
6. She's totally _____ . There's nothing in life she wants to do and nowhere she wants to go.
7. Jane's always happy and smiling. She's a _____ person.
8. Parents have to be _____ . Their children have to come first.
9. Henry's so sure about himself and what he can do. He's very _____ .
10. We have to invite Paula. It would be so _____ to invite her husband and not her.

Phrasal verbs

12 Phrasal verb + noun (1)

1 Many phrasal verbs go with a noun. Match a verb in **A** with a word or phrase in **B**.

A		B
1.	**b** turn on	a. clothes in a store
2.	☐ look after	b. a light
3.	☐ fill out	c. some information
4.	☐ find out	d. your coat
5.	☐ try on	e. the television at bedtime
6.	☐ look up	f. your parents
7.	☐ pick up	g. a form
8.	☐ take off	h. something you dropped
9.	☐ turn off	i. a word in the dictionary
10.	☐ get along with	j. the baby

2 Complete the sentences with the correct form of the phrasal verbs in Exercise 1.

1. **A** Can I ___try on___ these jeans, please?

   B Sure. The fitting rooms are over there.

2. I can't go out tonight. I'm _____ the children.

3. There's a show I want to watch. Can you _____ the TV?

4. No one's watching the TV. _____ it _____, please.

5. **A** What do I do with this form?

   B Just _____ it _____, and give it to the receptionist.

6. If there's a word I don't know, I _____ it _____ in my dictionary.

7. Please _____ your dirty shoes before you come in.

8. I _____ my sister but not my brother. We fight all the time.

9. Oh, no—I've dropped my purse. Could you _____ it _____ for me? Thanks.

10. **A** Can you _____ the time of the next train to New York?

    B OK. I'll look on the Internet.

Listening

13 What's cooking?

1 **CD1 12** Listen to Matt Greenberg, a TV chef. He's cooking a recipe for "Bread and Butter Pudding." Put a check (✓) next to the ingredients he uses in the recipe.

☐ 12 slices white bread, cut into triangles
☐ 8 egg yolks
☐ 4 Tbs unsalted butter
☐ 1 tsp salt
☐ 2 cups sugar
☐ a few drops vanilla extract
☐ ½ cup raisins
☐ 1 lemon
☐ 2 cups milk
☐ 5 cups flour
☐ 2 cups heavy cream
☐ 1 orange rind (grated)

2 Are the sentences true (✓) or false (✗)?

1. Matt works in a hotel kitchen.
2. He doesn't like running a kitchen because it's so stressful.
3. Many people think that British cooking is a little boring.
4. The recipe he's making today isn't expensive.
5. He's making the recipe slightly differently today.

3 Complete the lines from the show with the correct form of the verb in parentheses.

1. You _____ (come) from England originally, don't you?

2. I _____ (think) simple traditional cooking with the best ingredients is never boring.

3. So what _____ (you / make) for us today?

4. Now, I normally _____ (use) just raisins in this, but today I _____ (put) some fresh orange in as well.

5. Right, now I _____ (heat) the milk, cream, and vanilla in a pan …

6. These _____ (grow) in the Mediterranean.

7. Mmm, just the way I _____ (like) it.

8. Well, they _____ (not know) what they _____ (miss), do they?

CD1 12 Listen again and check.

3 Good times, bad times

Grammar: Past Simple and Continuous
– active and passive • Past Perfect •
Prepositions of time
Vocabulary: Birth, marriage, death
Pronunciation: Phonetic symbols;
consonants

Past tenses

1 Recognizing tenses

Read the text. Use the past verb forms in *italics*
to complete the chart.

Past Simple (x7)
felt

Past Continuous (x3)

Past Simple passive (x4)

Past Perfect (x3)

Past Perfect Continuous (x1)

Billionaire rips a hole in his Picasso worth $139 million

Steve Wynn, the billionaire art collector, *felt* extremely embarrassed
after he *had damaged* one of his own paintings by putting a hole in
the canvas.

Wynn, the 107th richest man in America, runs hotels and
casinos in Las Vegas. He owns a Matisse, a Renoir, a Van Gogh, a
Gauguin, and several Warhols.

He *bought* a Picasso, *Le Rêve (The Dream)* in 1997. It *was painted* in
1932, and it depicts Picasso's mistress as she is sitting daydreaming.
Wynn *paid* $48 million for it.

Despite being one of his favorite pictures, Wynn *had decided* to
sell it. He *had been negotiating* with an investor, Steven Cohen, and
they *had agreed* a price of $139 million.

The weekend before the sale, some friends of his *were visiting*
from New York, staying in one of his hotels. They *wanted* to see the
picture, which *was hanging* in his office, before it *was sold*. Wynn *was
standing* in front of the picture and explaining its history when he
accidentally *put* his elbow through the canvas.

The picture *was repaired* by an art restorer in New York. It is now
impossible to see where it *was damaged*. Not surprisingly, Cohen no
longer *wanted to* buy it, so Wynn *put* it in a vault for safe keeping.

2 Producing tenses

Use information from the text to complete the sentences with the correct form of the verb in **bold**. Use each form once.

paint — PAST SIMPLE or PAST SIMPLE PASSIVE?

1. Picasso _painted_ a picture of his mistress daydreaming.
2. *Le Rêve* _____ in 1932.

visit — PAST SIMPLE or PAST CONTINUOUS?

3. His New York friends _____ for the weekend.
4. They often _____ him in Las Vegas.

see — PAST SIMPLE or PAST PERFECT?

5. When his friends _____ the Picasso, they were amazed.
6. When his friends _____ the Picasso, they left the office.

put — PAST SIMPLE or PAST SIMPLE PASSIVE?

7. He _____ his elbow through the canvas.
8. *Le Rêve* _____ into a vault to keep it safe.

3 Questions

Write the questions.

1. _When did he buy the Picasso_ ?
   In 1997.
2. _____ ?
   In 1932.
3. _____ ?
   $48 million.
4. _____ hanging?
   In Wynn's office.
5. _____ ?
   By an art restorer in New York.

4 Negatives

Make these sentences negative.

1. *Le Rêve* was painted by Van Gogh.
   It wasn't painted by Van Gogh.

2. Wynn's friends were staying in his house.
   _____

3. They had seen the Picasso before.
   _____

4. Steven Cohen bought the Picasso.
   _____

5. Wynn sold it to someone else.
   _____

Past Simple and Continuous

5 *What was he doing? What did he do?*

Read the newspaper stories and answer the questions.

HERO SAVES MAN'S LIFE
Jack Easton, 38, was driving home from work at around 6:30 in the evening when he saw a yellow VW van, driven by Ken Sharpe, crash into a tree. Without thinking of his own safety, he pulled the young man out of the van and took him straight to the hospital. The doctors say Ken will make a complete recovery.

1. What was Jack Easton doing when he saw the accident?
   _____

2. What did he do when he saw the accident?
   _____

Dog attacked in park by swans
Hilary Benting, 54, was taking her dog, Toby, for a walk in City Park last Thursday afternoon. She was throwing sticks into the pond for Toby to retrieve. He was swimming in the pond when he was attacked by two swans. He received cuts and bruises. Mrs. Benting called park officials to help, but there was little they could do.

3. What was Mrs. Benting doing when her dog was attacked? What was Toby doing?
   _____

4. What did she do when her dog was attacked?
   _____

Shock for bank customers
■ Customers in the Whitehall Savings Bank were shocked yesterday as they were standing in a line talking to each other. At 11:15 two masked robbers burst into the bank carrying shotguns. Sixty-year-old Martin Webb suffered a heart attack and was taken to the hospital. The robbers escaped with $800,000.

5. What was happening in the bank when the robbers burst in?
   _____

6. What happened to Martin Webb when the robbers burst in?
   _____

Past Perfect

6 What had happened?

Complete the sentences. Use the prompts in parentheses and the Past Perfect.

1. I was broke because I __'d spent all my money on clothes__ .
   (spend / money / clothes)

2. Jane was furious because she _____
   _____ . (oversleep / miss the bus)

3. Mary was very disappointed with her son. He
   _____ . (not study
   enough / fail exams)

4. Before his accident, Peter _____
   _____ . (be / best player / team)

5. I was nervous as I waited at the gate.
   I _____ .
   (never / fly / before)

6. Jack wanted a new challenge in his work.
   He _____ .
   (do / same job / ten years) (CONTINUOUS)

7 Past Simple or Past Perfect?

Circle the correct tenses in the story.

A Busy Day

It was ten o'clock in the evening. Peter (1) _sat_ / had sat
down on his sofa and thought about the day. What a
busy day it (2) _was_ / had been! This was his first night in his
own apartment. He (3) _lived_ / had lived his whole life with
his family, and now for the first time, he (4) _was_ / had been
on his own.

He sat surrounded by boxes that he (5) _didn't manage_ /
hadn't managed to unpack during the day. It (6) _took_ / had
taken months to get all his things together. His mother
(7) _was_ / had been very generous, buying him things like
towels and mugs.

He (8) _went_ / had gone into the kitchen and (9) _made_ /
had made a sandwich. He suddenly (10) _felt_ / had felt very
tired and yawned. No wonder he (11) _was_ / had been tired!
He (12) _was_ / had been up since six o'clock in
the morning. He (13) _decided_ / had decided to
eat his sandwich and go to bed. But he
didn't make it. He sat down on
his sofa, and before he knew it,
he (14) _was_ / had been fast asleep.

Tense review

8 ate, was eating, or had eaten?

Put the verb in **bold** in the Past Simple, Past Continuous, or Past Perfect.

`eat`

1. I couldn't understand what she was saying because
   she __was eating__ an apple.

2. The meal was terrible, but John _____ it all up.
   He must have been hungry.

3. There was nothing in the fridge. The kids
   _____ everything.

`talk`

4. The class was so boring. The teacher just
   _____ for a whole hour.

5. I knew about Annie's problem because I _____
   to her mother the day before.

6. Who _____ you _____ to on the phone
   just now?

`drive`

7. "How did you get here?" "I _____ ."

8. I was tired and needed to go to bed. I _____
   300 miles that day.

9. I _____ to work when I had an accident and
   hit a tree.

Past passive

9 Past Simple passive

Put the verbs in parentheses in the Past Simple passive.

1. _Romeo and Juliet_ __was written__ (write) in 1595 or 1596.

2. It _____ (base) on a traditional Italian tale.

3. It isn't known when it _____ first _____
   (perform).

4. The play _____ (publish) in 1597.

5. Many of Shakespeare's plays _____ (perform)
   at the Globe Theatre in London.

6. The original theater _____ (build) in 1599.

7. The theater _____ (destroy) by fire in 1613.

8. The 1996 movie version, starring Leonardo di Caprio,
   _____ (aim) at a younger audience.

9. The movie _____ (shoot) in Mexico City.

10. The musical and movie _West Side Story_ _____
    (inspire) by Shakespeare's play.

Love on the tube

10 Questions and negatives

Read the first newspaper article.
Complete the questions.

1. When __was she visiting New York__ ?
   Last year.

2. Who _____ ?
   A young commuter.

3. What _____ doing?
   Listening to his MP3 player.

4. Why _____ ?
   Because she was too shy.

5. Which train _____ ?
   The 6 train.

6. Where _____ ?
   At 42nd Street.

Read the second article.
Complete the negative sentences.

7. She / not see / the man since November.
   She hadn't seen the man since November.

8. She / not receive / any replies on the Internet.
   _____

9. Mr. Laurence / not sit / on the subway.
   _____

10. He / not buy / a copy of the newspaper.
    _____

11. He / not know / why people were looking at him.
    _____

12. Mr. Laurence / not go out / with anyone.
    _____

Read the third article.
Complete the text using the verbs from the box.

got	went	met
had	enjoyed	did
was looking	had invited	

THURSDAY, JANUARY 11

Girl looks for love on the subway

Jana Ohlson was visiting New York last (1) ▓▓▓ when she saw (2) ▓▓▓ on the subway. He was (3) ▓▓▓. She didn't talk to him because (4) ▓▓▓. However, she *did* take his photograph on her cell phone. She went back to Sweden but couldn't forget the handsome man she'd seen on the subway, so she put his photo and a message on the Internet.

The mystery man was traveling on the (5) ▓▓▓ train and got off at (6) ▓▓▓ at about 5:30 p.m.

■ If you know the man, or are him, call *City News* at (212) 555-6439.

The mystery man

FRIDAY, JANUARY 12

Tourist finds her mystery man

City News has ended the love search of a Swedish tourist. Jana Ohlson had been looking for a young man she'd seen last November on the New York City subway.

Jana put his photo on the Internet, but no one replied. His picture appeared in yesterday's paper, and he was identified as Sam Laurence, a financial adviser from Tribeca. His work colleagues contacted *City News*.

Mr. Laurence said, "I'd already seen the photo on my way to work. I was standing on the train reading the paper over someone's shoulder. I couldn't understand why people were giving me funny looks."

Miss Ohlson was very pleased to learn that Mr. Laurence didn't have a girlfriend.

Jana Ohlson in Sweden yesterday

WEDNESDAY, FEBRUARY 7

Couple delighted with Internet date

The couple who (13) _____ after an international search on the Internet have had their first date.

Sam Laurence, 28, and Jana Ohlson, 25, from Uppsala, (14) _____ a sightseeing tour of New York and then (15) _____ lunch in the West Village.

He said, "It (16) _____ very well. We had a lot of fun, and we really (17) _____ ourselves. We (18) _____ along really well."

Miss Ohlson said that she (19) _____ Sam to go to Sweden, and that she (20) _____ forward to showing him her hometown.

Vocabulary

11 Birth, marriage, and death

> **!** 1 The verb *marry* is used without a preposition.
> *My sister **married** a plumber.*
>
> 2 *Get married* refers to the change of state between being single and being married.
> *We **got married** in 2002.*
>
> 3 *Married* refers to the state.
> *Is your brother **married**?*
>
> 4 *Get married* and *be married* can both be used with the preposition *to*.
> *She **got married to** Gary last weekend.*
> *My sister **is married to** a really nice guy.*

1 Complete the sentences with a word from the box.

birth	birthday	born

1. Where were you _____ ?
2. When is your _____ ?
3. She gave _____ to a beautiful healthy boy.
4. (*On an official form*) Date of _____
5. Congratulations on the _____ of little Albert.
6. What are you doing for your _____ this year?

2 Complete the sentences with the words from the box.

get married	marry	married	got married
been married	wedding	marriage	

1. **A** Are you _____ ?
   B No, I'm single. But I'd like to _____ someday.
2. Darling, I love you. Will you _____ me?
3. How many times has she _____ ?
4. We're engaged, and we're going to _____ next fall.
5. My wife and I have _____ for twenty-five years.
6. We had a lovely _____ in a small country inn.
7. Did you hear? James and Sue _____ last week.
8. Their _____ was always perfect until the end.

3 Complete the sentences with a word from the box.

dying	dead	died	death	die

1. Shakespeare _____ in 1616.
2. Julius Caesar was stabbed to _____ by his best friend, Brutus.
3. **A** Is old Bertie Harrison still alive?
   B I'm sure he's _____ . Didn't he _____ a few years ago?
4. Her father's _____ came as a great shock. He _____ of a heart attack.
5. She screamed when she saw the _____ mouse on the floor.
6. Our poor old cat is _____ . We've had her for fifteen years. She just sleeps all day long.
7. Every winter thousands of birds _____ in the cold weather.
8. Those flowers have _____ . Throw them away.

Prepositions

12 *in / at / on* for time

Complete the sentences with *in, at, on,* or – (no preposition).

1. **A** What did you do ___ last weekend?

   B ___ Friday evening we went to a party. We slept late ___ Saturday morning, and then ___ the afternoon we went shopping. ___ seven o'clock some friends came over for dinner. We didn't do much ___ Sunday—___ the evening we just watched TV. What about you?

2. I'll call you ___ next week ___ Thursday. It'll probably be ___ the afternoon ___ about 3:00 p.m. OK?

3. I don't see my parents much. ___ Thanksgiving Day, usually, and ___ the summer.

4. ___ November 9th, 1989, the Berlin Wall was opened. For the first time ___ the late twentieth century Germans could go from West to East Berlin without travel restrictions.

5. **A** You look tired. What were you doing ___ last night?

   B I was trying to finish my History essay. I'm having to work a lot ___ night lately. It has to be handed in ___ this Friday, and I still have a lot to write.

   A Oh well, I'll see you ___ lunchtime—if you're still awake.

6. The weather in New York is unreliable. ___ summer it can be very hot, but it often rains ___ April and June. The summer was awful ___ last year. The best weather is usually ___ spring and fall.

---

 1 We use *at* for times and certain expressions.
   at 8:00
   at midnight
   at lunchtime
   at the moment

2 We use *on* for days and dates.
   on Friday
   on Friday morning
   on September 12th
   on Saturday evening

3 We use *in* for longer periods such as months, seasons, and years.
   in April
   in 2002
   in the summer
   in the nineteenth century

4 We also use *in* for parts of the day.
   in the morning
   in the afternoon
   in the evening (but **at** night)

5 There is no preposition before *last, next, this,* or *tomorrow.*
   Did you go out **last** night?
   We're going away **this** weekend.
   I'll see you **next** week.
   Can you call me **tomorrow** morning?

Pronunciation

13 Phonetic symbols – consonants

1 Many phonetic symbols for consonants are easy.

/b/	/k/	/r/	/d/
/bɪg/ big	/kæn/ can	/rʌn/ run	/du/ do

/l/	/s/	/y/	
/lɪv/ live	/sɪt/ sit	/yes/ yes	

CD1 13 Listen and repeat.

2 These symbols are less obvious.

/θ/	/ð/	/ʃ/	/ʒ/
/θɪŋk/ think	/ðoʊz/ those	/ʃʊd/ should	/tɛləvɪʒn/ television/

/tʃ/	/dʒ/	/ŋ/	
/watʃ/ watch	/dʒʌst/ just	/brɪŋ/ bring	

CD1 14 Listen and repeat.

3 Write the words in the correct box according to the sound underlined.

thought	tongue	this	age	machine
bath	mature	lunch	share	measure
weather	bank	gadget	pleasure	mother
fetch	thanks	German	wash	hang
revision				

/θ/	/tʃ/	/ʃ/
_____	_____	_____
_____	_____	_____
_____	_____	_____

/ð/	/dʒ/	/ʒ/
_____	_____	_____
_____	_____	_____
_____	_____	_____

/ŋ/
_____
_____
_____

CD1 15 Listen, check, and repeat.

▶▶ **Phonetic symbols p. 93**

Listening

14 Memories

1 **CD1 16** Listen to three friends, Carol, Anne, and Richard, talking about their earliest memories. What is each person's earliest memory?

Carol _____

Anne _____

Richard _____

2 Answer the questions.
1. Why did Carol love sitting on her father's shoulders?
2. Why didn't her father want to carry her on the day she remembers?
3. Why is this memory so important in her life?
4. How does Anne know that she didn't invent her memory?
5. How long was it before her family used the Christmas tree the second time?
6. What does Carol think Anne's memory shows?

3 **CD1 16** Listen again and complete the extracts from the conversation.

1. My mom says my dad _____ me a lot on his shoulders at that age, and I absolutely _____ it because he _____ a really big, tall man.

2. That's of this one day when I _____ with my mom and dad, and older sister. We _____ through some fields near where we _____ , and my dad _____ pick me up.

3. Well I know this isn't something _____ because when I _____ my mom, she _____ like that.

4 Getting it right

Modal and related verbs

1 Recognizing verb forms

Read the text. Use the verb forms in *italics* to complete the chart.

Things that are IMPORTANT to do	
with *have to*	have to buy
with *must*	

Things that are IMPORTANT NOT to do	
with *shouldn't*	

Things that are NOT NECESSARY to do	
with *don't have to*	

Things that are A GOOD IDEA to do	
with *should*	

Things that you are ABLE or PERMITTED to do	
with *can*	

Things that are FORBIDDEN to do	
with *can't*	
with *not allowed to*	

Tips for visitors to the U.S.

The weather You *should check* the weather before you come. The weather varies from region to region.

Food and drink In most coffee shops you *have to buy* your drink at the counter, then carry your drink to a table. You are usually served at a table in a nice cafe or restaurant.

Tipping is a problem. You *don't have to leave* a tip in a coffee shop, but in a restaurant you *should leave* about 15–20%. Similarly you *can tip* a taxi driver if you want.

In a restaurant, you *shouldn't say* "Give me the menu!" or "I want some water!" This is considered very rude. You *should be* polite and say "Could I have the menu, please." We tend to say "Please" and "Thank you" a lot.

People You *shouldn't address* people as "Mr." or "Mrs." We usually say: "Good morning," not "Good morning, Mr."

Transportation Obviously, you *have to have* a driver's license to rent a car, and the law says you *must wear* a seat belt in the back seat as well as the front. In some states, you *aren't allowed to use* your cell phone while driving.

Tourism In New York, you *should buy* a MetroCard. With this you *can travel* on the subway and the buses.

You *have to pay* to visit most museums and art galleries.

You *must see* Grand Central Terminal, the Empire State Building, and Central Park. They're too good to miss.

General You *can get* cash from ATM machines, which are everywhere.

You *aren't allowed to smoke* in any public buildings. You *can't smoke* in restaurants.

Obligation

2 have to/don't have to

Look at the photos. Match the sentences with the people.

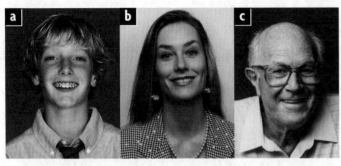

1. [b] I have to wear business casual attire.
2. [ ] I always have to be home before 11:00 P.M.
3. [ ] My dad usually has to work in the evenings.
4. [ ] I don't have to get up at 6:30 A.M. anymore.
5. [ ] My husband has to take our children to school every morning.
6. [ ] My wife has to go to the hospital every week.
7. [ ] I have to get good grades this semester.
8. [ ] My little sister doesn't have to help with the housework.
9. [ ] I often have to travel abroad.

3 Questions with have to

Write the questions for these answers.

1. Why __does she have to__ wear business casual attire?
   Because she has to meet a lot of important people.
2. Why _____ be home before 11:00 P.M.?
   Because his parents say that he has to.
3. Why _____ work in the evenings?
   Because he's a teacher, and he has to prepare lessons.
4. Why _____ get up at 6:30 A.M.?
   Because he's retired.
5. Why _____ go to the hospital?
   Because she broke her arm, and she has to have physiotherapy.
6. Why _____ get good grades this semester?
   Because he wants to go to Oxford University.
7. Why _____ help with the housework?
   Because her mother says that she is still too young.
8. Why _____ travel abroad?
   Because she works for an international company.

4 Forms of have to

Match a line in **A** with a line in **B**.

A
1. [ ] I don't have to get up early tomorrow …
2. [ ] My grandmother had to go to work …
3. [ ] We're having to economize …
4. [ ] You'll have to study hard …
5. [ ] You didn't have to buy me a present, …
6. [ ] Will I have to take the exam again …

B
a. if you want to be a doctor.
b. because it's the weekend.
c. if I don't pass?
d. when she was just 12.
e. because we're saving up for a vacation.
f. but it was very kind of you.

5 must and have to

> ❗ There is a difference between *must* and *have to*.
> *Must* expresses the authority of the speaker.
> *Have to* refers to the authority of another person, or to obligation generally.
> If you are not sure which one to use to express obligation, use *have to*.

Match the pairs of sentences with their meaning.

1. I must have a drink of water. [b]
   I have to drink lots of water. [a]

   a. The doctor told me to.
   b. I'm really thirsty.

2. I must do my homework tonight. [ ]
   I have to do my homework tonight. [ ]

   c. I'm telling myself it's important.
   d. That's why I can't come out with you tonight.

3. We must go to Paris some time. [ ]
   We have to go to Paris next week. [ ]

   e. Another boring business trip! Yawn!
   f. It would be so romantic!

4. I must water the plants today. [ ]
   I have to water the plants today. [ ]

   g. I haven't done them for ages.
   h. They need lots and lots of water.

5. We must have lunch soon. [ ]
   We have to have lunch with our boss. [ ]

   i. What about next Wednesday?
   j. We better look sharp!

6 Talking about obligation

Complete the sentences with *must*, *have to*, or *had to*.

a "You _____ be home by 11:00."

b "Bye! Dad said I _____ be home by 11:00."

a "You _____ stay in bed for a few days."

b "The doctor told me I _____ stay in bed for a few days."

a "I _____ wash my hair tonight."

b "I _____ wash all these dishes."

a "I _____ go and see the doctor."

b "Sorry, I _____ go to the doctor at 3 P.M."

7 *shouldn't / don't have to / didn't have to*

Choose the correct verb form.

1. We have a lot to do tomorrow. You *shouldn't* / *don't have to* go out tonight.
2. You *shouldn't* / *don't have to* tell Mary what I told you. It's a secret.
3. The museum is free. You *shouldn't* / *don't have to* pay to get in.
4. In the 19th century children *shouldn't* / *didn't have to* attend school up to the age of 16.
5. Terry's a millionaire. He *shouldn't* / *doesn't have to* go to work.
6. When I was a child I *didn't have to* / *don't have to* do my dishes. My mother did it for me.
7. We *shouldn't* / *don't have to* rush. We have plenty of time.
8. You *shouldn't* / *don't have to* play with knives. They're dangerous.
9. This is my favorite pen. You can borrow it, but you *shouldn't* / *don't have to* lose it.
10. **A** Should I come with you?
    B You can if you want, but you *shouldn't* / *don't have to*.

8 *should* for advice

1 Read the sentences. Give advice using *should* and an idea from the box.

do more exercise	~~let him play for an hour~~
take up a sport or a hobby	get it serviced

1. My son never wants to go out, he just plays computer games all day!

   You <u>should let him play for an hour</u> , and then tell him to stop and do something else.

2. My car keeps breaking down.

   _____ .

3. My wife isn't sleeping very well these days.

   _____ .

4. Since he retired, my father doesn't know what to do with himself.

   _____ .

2 Complete the questions with *do you think I should …?* and an idea from the box.

go to	~~go out with~~	say	take	have

1. Peter wants to go out with me. He's nice, but I only like him as a friend.

   <u>Do you think I should go out with</u> him?

2. I've been offered admission to Columbia and Harvard.

   Which university _____?

3. Everything on the menu looks wonderful!

   What _____?

4. I have a terrible headache, and I can't read the instructions on this aspirin bottle.

   How many _____?

5. My aunt has invited me to her picnic, but I don't want to go.

   What _____ to her?

9 Modern manners

Do the quiz to see if you know how to behave!

Do **you** have good manners?

Choose the response that's true for you.

1. You're in a restaurant with friends and your cell phone rings. Should you …
   a. answer it in front of them?
   b. turn your phone off, of course?

2. You get a present for your birthday. You need to say thank you. Should you …
   a. text?
   b. e-mail?

3. You are at the dinner table. Your meal has arrived, but no one else's has. Should you …
   a. start eating?
   b. wait for everyone else to be served?

4. You've been invited to dinner. Should you take …
   a. homemade baked goods?
   b. something to offer — some flowers, a box of chocolates?

5. You get an invitation to the kind of evening you really can't stand. Should you …
   a. ignore the invitation?
   b. make up an excuse?

6. Your friend asks if you like his/her new clothes. You think they're awful. Should you …
   a. tell the truth?
   b. say they look great?

7. You're at home watching your favorite TV show when some friends arrive. Should you …
   a. invite your friends to watch with you?
   b. turn off the TV?

8. You're on the bus listening to your MP3 player. Someone asks you to turn it down. Should you …
   a. pay no attention and carry on listening?
   b. apologize and turn it down?

Of course it's impossible to say what is the correct way to behave in all situations. The more polite answers are probably **b**, the more impolite **a**.

1. Young people think it's OK to leave their phones on. Older people find this very rude.
2. An e-mail saying thank you is probably fine.
3. **a** is very impolite.
4. Either is fine.
5. **b** is probably what most people do if they really don't want to go.
6. It depends how well you know your friend.
7. Some people have no hesitation in keeping on the TV. For others this is incredibly rude.
8. **b** is the polite thing to do.

Permission and ability

10 can and be allowed to

Who says these sentences? Where?

1. "You can't park here. I'll have to give you a parking ticket."

   <u>A police officer in the street.</u>

2. "I'm sorry, sir, but you can't get on the plane without a passport."

   _____

3. "You aren't allowed to look at your notes during the exam."

   _____

4. "Shh! You can't talk in here. People are studying."

   _____

5. "You can take your seat belt off now. You still aren't allowed to use personal computers or cell phones."

   _____

6. "We're allowed to make one phone call a week, and we can go to the library, but we spend most of our time in our cells."

   _____

7. "You can take photographs, but you can't use flash or touch any of the exhibits."

   _____

8. "You aren't allowed to jump into the pool, but you can use the diving board at the deep end."

   _____

Obligation and permission

11 The pain and pleasure of being a teenager

Complete the interview with Ana and Ben with the correct form of *can*, *be allowed to*, or *have to*.

Interviewer What are some of the good things about being a teenager and not an adult?

Ana Well, we (1) _____ earn a living for a start.

Ben We (2) _____ go out with our friends, go shopping, go to the movies.

I So what you're saying is, what's good is that you have no responsibilities?

A Yeah, we're pretty free. We (3) _____ do what we like, most of the time.

B But money's a problem. What's good is that you (4) _____ pay bills, but it also means we can't buy what we want.

A Yes, we never have enough money.

I What do you think it's like being an adult?

A Well, adults have to worry about bills so they (5) _____ earn a living. They don't have as much free time as we do. They're always busy. They (6) _____ do what they want, when they want.

I Who do you feel more sorry for, your mom or your dad?

B My mom. She looks after us kids, take us to school and swimming and dance, and she goes to work. And she (7) _____ cook, clean, and run the house.

A I feel more sorry for my dad. He (8) _____ travel a lot, so we go weeks without seeing him, *and* that's really tough on him and us.

B But the very worst thing about being a teenager is that we have to go to school.

I Is that so bad?

A Yes! The rules are so stupid! There are certain clothes we (9) _____ wear, like short skirts or ripped jeans.

I What's so bad? I (10) _____ wear a stupid hat when I was at school!

B And you (11) _____ do so much homework.

A And you can't skip class and (12) you _____ use your cell phone!

I Oh! What a difficult life you two lead!

Phrasal verbs

12 Separable or inseparable?

1 Put the noun in parentheses in two places in these sentences.

1. Could you turn / off (the light)?
   <u>Could you turn the light off?</u>   <u>Could you turn off the light?</u>

2. Look at the trash on the street! I have to pick / up (those empty bottles)!

   _____

3. I saw some beautiful clothes today. I tried / on (a coat), but I didn't buy it.

   _____

   _____

4. Please don't throw / away (those newspapers). I haven't read them yet.

   _____

   _____

5. I'll sort / out (this problem). Don't you worry about it.

   _____

   _____

2 Rewrite the sentences in the exercise above with the noun as a pronoun.

1. <u>Could you turn it off?</u>   4. _____

2. <u>I have to pick them up.</u>   5. _____

3. _____

3 Put the nouns in parentheses in just one place in these sentences.

1. I'm looking for (Peter – him).
   <u>I'm looking for Peter.</u>   <u>I'm looking for him.</u>

2. When you get to the reception, ask for (Mr. Smith. – me).

   _____

   _____

3. I'm looking forward to (the party – it).

   _____

   _____

4. You go out tonight. I'll look after (the children – them).

   _____

   _____

5. I like my husband's family. I get along well with (my mother-in-law – her).

   _____

   _____

Listening

13 A radio call-in

1 Listen to a radio call-in about "rules that were made to be broken." There are three topics discussed:

a. Table manners   **b.** School rules   **c.** Driving rules

Which topics do you think these lines from the call-in refer to? Put a, b, or c.

1. [a] You shouldn't put your elbows on the table.
2. [ ] … you have to have some way of showing responsibility.
3. [ ] They're saying you shouldn't eat at the wheel, aren't they?
4. [ ] Why aren't I allowed to leave school to have lunch?
5. [ ] Apparently you shouldn't read a map or talk to a passenger.
6. [ ] … you have to eat up everything on your plate.

CD1 17 Listen and check.

2 Choose the correct answer.

1. Tony thinks you can eat more *quickly / easily* with your elbows on the table.
2. He says we teach children to eat *too quickly / too much*.
3. Sarah wants to *stay in / leave* school to have lunch.
4. She thinks *older / younger* students should be allowed to leave school if they want to.
5. Andy explains that it's only *using a cell phone / eating at the wheel* that's actually illegal.
6. He thinks that changing CDs while you're driving is *less / more* dangerous than talking to someone.

3 Complete these lines from the call-in with the correct form of the phrasal verb from the box.

come up to	cut off	get through	pick up

1. "And it's just _____ ten minutes to nine."
2. "I think people just _____ these rules from their parents."
3. "Can you hear me? Oh, I'm sorry, it looks like Sarah's been _____ ."
4. "… do try calling again if you don't _____ the first time."

CD1 17 Listen again and check.

Vocabulary Crossword 1

Use the clues to complete the crossword. All these words and expressions have appeared in Units 1–4.

ACROSS

4. Juliet was very _____ when she heard Romeo's family name. (5)
6. The number of people living in a country is the _____ . (10)
8. A _____ is someone who doesn't eat meat. (10)
10. Most of the world's _____ comes from Saudi Arabia. (3)
13. Her health has picked up since she moved to a country with a sunny _____ . (7)
14. When something is _____ , it's very, very old. (7)
15. The _____ for Boniface's apartment is $45 a month. (4)
16. Someone who is no longer married is _____ . (8)
19. In the U.S. you have to be 18 years old to _____ military service. (2)
20. The Gregory family live in a _____ house (big). (5)
21. A _____ is someone who looks after people in a hospital. (5)
24. "What's the telephone area _____ for New York?" "It's 212." (4)
25. _____ is another word for "frightening." (5)
27. The Gregory children learned to appreciate small _____ . (6)
28. The Qu family motto is "save money, live simply, care _____ your friends." (3)
29. The Gregory children have _____ bedrooms, full of expensive things. (4)
32. Joaquim is here _____ a business trip. (2)
33. A _____ is a very bad or frightening dream. (9)
34. You have to wear a seat _____ when you're driving. (4)
35. A country whose Head of State is a king or queen, like the UK or Spain, is a _____ . (8)

DOWN

1. Someone or something from a different country is _____ . (7)
2. English people usually call an "apartment" a _____ . (4)
3. The _____ of *Romeo and Juliet* has a very sad ending. (5)
4. Romeo went to the Capulet's party _____ (without an invitation). (9)
5. "I guess he's married." "I think _____ too." (I agree). (2)
7. If something is against the law, it is _____ . (7)
9. Mmm! Are these potatoes fried, or _____ in the oven? (7)
11. How long does _____ take you to get to school? (2)
12. Someone who can speak two languages is _____ . (9)
15. An HR manager has to _____ new staff. (7)
17. I _____ out of gas on the way home! I had to walk to the garage. (3)
18. Charles and Camilla are both _____ about hunting (have strong feelings about.) (10)
22. If you act very strangely and differently from other people, they think you are _____ . (9)
23. That's the Manager, and that's her _____ Assistant, answering her calls. (8)
26. As a _____ man, van Gogh worked in London and Paris. (5)
30. We're just having dinner. Have you _____ yet? (5)
31. The people in a close-_____ family have strong relationships with each other. (4)

5 Our changing world

Future forms

1 Recognizing tenses

Read the text. Use the future verb forms in *italics* to complete the chart.

prediction with *will* (x 3)   prediction with *won't* (x 2)
will be
prediction with *going to* (x 2)   intention with *going to* (x 1)
arrangement with Present Continuous (x 2)
possibility with *may* (x 2)
possibility with *might* (x 2)
possibility with *could* (x 1)

LONG HOT SUMMER FOR AUSTRALIAN FARMERS

Sydney — Paddy Carrigan's family has been farming near Grenfell, 233 miles north of Sydney, for 120 years. This *will be* the first year when there hasn't been a harvest. It hasn't rained for five years. He looks up at the cloudless sky and sighs. "And it looks like it's *going to be* another long, dry summer."

Generations of Sally Young's family have been born on her farm in Wakool. The family *is moving* to Melbourne next month. "We*'re going to live* with my husband's family. We just can't stay here any longer. It's very sad. My children *won't grow up* here."

Malcolm Adlington has a dairy farm close to the Murray River. "I*'m getting rid of* my herd in the next couple of weeks. I'm in so much debt that I*'m going to have to* sell my farm."

The drought is Australia's worst in a century. Economist Justin Smirk says that production of wheat and rice *might fall* by as much as 20 percent. He believes the drought *will change* agricultural practices forever. "It *won't be* easy to grow crops such as rice in the future. We *might have to* stop farming in very dry areas."

Despite the signs, the government refuses to blame the drought on climate change. But scientist Peter Cullen is more certain. "Many of our agricultural areas *will become* hotter and drier. They *may stop* producing crops altogether. This *could be* the end for some of Australia's 100,000 farming businesses. People now working on the land *may have to* take up more productive jobs in the cities."

will

2 Predictions

Write the sentences with *will* and the prompts.

1. You've been studying so hard.
   I / sure / you / pass / exam.
   I'm sure you'll pass your exam.

2. I think / go / bed soon. I have to be up early tomorrow.
   _____

3. You don't need your umbrella. I / not / think / it / rain today.
   _____

4. I'm going to an elegant restaurant tonight. I wonder if / I / meet anyone famous.
   _____

5. You could ask Jack for some money, but I / not / think / he / lend you any.
   _____

6. Are you seeing that new movie tonight?
   I / sure / you / not / like it. It's very violent.
   _____

7. I'll have some soup ready for you. I expect you / be / hungry after your trip.
   _____

8. It's a good idea, but I / not think / it / work.
   _____

3 Questions and negatives

Write the questions with *will* and the prompts in parentheses.

1. So you're going on vacation! (When / back?)
   When will you be back?

2. So you finished your exams. (When / results?)
   _____

3. So you ran out of money! (How / pay bills?)
   _____

4. So you're going to live on an island! (What / eat?)
   _____

5. So Peter's giving you a ride to the party! (How / home?)
   _____

Complete the negatives with *won't* to express the same idea.

6. I'll pass.
   I won't fail.

7. They'll arrive on time.
   _____ be late.

8. He'll remember your birthday.
   _____

9. You'll hate the movie.
   _____ enjoy the movie.

10. Brazil will win the game.

4 Offering to help

Make offers with *I'll*.

1. It's so hot in here!
   I'll open the window.

2. I'm so thirsty.
   _____

3. There's someone at the door.
   _____

4. I don't have any money.
   _____

5. I can't do the homework.
   _____

going to

5 What's going to happen?

Look at the pictures. Write what is going to happen.

He's going to get a haircut.
_____
_____

_____
_____
_____

will or going to?

6 Planned or spontaneous?

Complete the conversations with *will* or *going to* and the verb in parentheses. Use the most natural form.

1. **A** Why are you wearing your old clothes?

   B Because I _'m going to wash_ (wash) the car.

2. **A** I have a headache. Do you have any aspirin?

   B Yes, they're in the bathroom. I _____ (get) some for you.

3. **A** Don't forget to tell me if I can help you.

   B Thank you. I _____ (give) you a call if I think of anything.

4. **A** Why are you making sandwiches?

   B Because we _____ (have) a picnic on the beach.

   A What a great idea! I _____ (get) the towels and the swimsuits.

5. **A** I'm going now! Bye!

   B Bye! What time _____ you _____ (be) back tonight?

   A I don't know. I _____ (call) you later.

6. **A** You still have my CD. Did you forget?

   B I'm sorry. Yes, I forgot. I _____ (give) it back to you tomorrow.

7. **A** Dad, can you lend me $10, please? I _____ (give) it back tomorrow.

   B I don't know. What _____ you _____ (do)?

   A I _____ (see) a movie with Tina and Mike.

8. **A** Your exams start in two weeks. When _____ you _____ (start) studying? You haven't started studying yet.

   B I know. I _____ (study) tonight.

   A You're going out tonight.

   B I _____ (start) tomorrow night, then.

Present Continuous

7 Making arrangements

Complete the conversation with the Present Continuous form of the verbs in the box.

invite	come	~~have~~	make	stay
get	bring	give	travel	deliver

A Can you keep a secret?

B Yes, of course. What is it?

A (1) **I'm having** a surprise party for Rosa next Saturday. It's her thirtieth birthday.

B A surprise party! That'll be difficult to arrange without her knowing. Who (2) _____ you _____ ?

A Everybody. All our friends, her friends from work, all her family, even two aunts from Mexico. They (3) _____ up on Friday evening and they (4) _____ with cousins.

B What about the food and drinks? Where (5) _____ you _____ that from?

A It's all arranged. Marcello's restaurant (6) _____ all kinds of food on Saturday afternoon, and their chef (7) _____ even _____ a special birthday cake with pink icing and sugar flowers.

B Excellent! And what (8) _____ you _____ Rosa for her birthday? Did you get her a good present?

A Oh yes! I booked a very special vacation. A week for two in Bali! We (9) _____ first class, and we (10) _____ in a five-star hotel.

B That's a great idea. Very nice! I can see that you're going to enjoy her birthday, too! Am I invited to this party?

A Of course. But keep it a secret!

CD1 18 Listen and check.

Expressing the future

8 *will*, *going to*, or the Present Continuous?

Choose the correct form of the verb.

1. **A** Do you have a toothache again?
   B Oooh! It's agony! But I *see / 'm seeing* the dentist this afternoon.

2. **A** Have you booked your vacation?
   B Yes, we have. We *'re going / 'll go* to Thailand.

3. **A** What a beautiful day! Not a cloud in the sky!
   B But the weather forecast says it's *raining / 's going to rain.*

4. **A** Please don't tell anyone. It's a secret.
   B Don't worry. We *won't tell / 're not telling* anybody.

5. **A** I don't have enough money to pay for my ticket.
   B It's OK. I'm *going to lend / 'll lend* you some.

6. **A** You two look really shocked. What's the matter?
   B We just found out that we *'ll have / 're having* twins!

7. **A** I thought you'd just bought a new dishwasher.
   B We did. It's *being / will be delivered* tomorrow.

8. **A** Can you meet me after work?
   B I'd love to, but John's *taking / 'll take* me out for dinner tonight.

may / might / could for possibility

9 *We may go to Thailand*

Complete the sentences using the prompts.

1. We haven't decided what we're doing this summer.
   (may – go to Thailand / Hawaii)
   We may go to Thailand, or we may go to Hawaii.

2. Let's go and see that new movie.
   (could – be good / be terrible)
   _____

3. Kate doesn't know what she wants to do when she grows up.
   (might – be a doctor / vet)
   _____

4. I can't decide which car I want.
   (may – buy a Ford / Toyota)
   _____

5. There are two things I'd like to see on TV tonight.
   (could – watch a movie / the game)
   _____

All future forms

10 The lottery winner

1 Complete the text about the lottery winner using the future verb forms a–l.

a. are getting married	**d.** may also buy	**g.** 're staying	**j.** 're flying
b̶. will change	**e.** 'm going to continue	**h.** 're going to see	**k.** won't be
c. 're going to make	**f.** 'll pay off	**i.** might treat ourselves	**l.** could get

Lottery winner Mandy is off to see the world

A Virginia hairdresser is celebrating in style after winning more than $1.5 million on the lottery.

Mandy Jones, 47, from Arlington, Virginia, discovered her win on Monday. "I'm absolutely thrilled," she said. "I've been playing the lottery for a long time, but I've never won anything until now."

Mrs. Jones doesn't think that the win (1) _b_ her life at all. "I'm still the same person. I have no plans to quit my job. I (2) ___ being a hairdresser because I like the people I work with."

Husband Alan, 52, an electrician, said, "I'm going to be self-employed. I've always wanted to work for myself. Now I can do it."

Mrs. Jones and her husband plan to invest some of the money, but they also intend to enjoy their new-found wealth.

Mrs. Jones said, "We (3) ___ sure our children are secure, and then we're going to do some traveling. First we (4) ___ to New York for a week, and we (5) ___ in the Plaza Hotel on Central Park. Then we (6) ___ the Terracotta Army in China. It's something I've always wanted to do."

Daughter Helen, 21, and son Mike, 18, are less enthusiastic about the Terracotta Army, but they have each been promised a little something of their own.

"I'm getting a car on Saturday," said Mike. "I want a Jeep. A blue one."

The couple are buying a new house for Helen. She said, "I've already chosen the house. I have lots of plans. My boyfriend and I (7) ___ next spring, so this win couldn't have come at a better time for us."

Mr. and Mrs. Jones (8) ___ a new house for themselves, but it (9) ___ far away from where they live now. "We (10) ___ ourselves to a house with a double garage. Right now we only have a single garage," said Mrs. Jones.

Celebrating in the gardens of the Inn at Little Washington, Mr. Jones said, "Of course we've always had money problems, but now things (11) ___ easier. People say money can't buy you happiness, but it sure helps. I think we (12) ___ our credit card bills and then see what's best to do after that."

2 Here are the answers to some questions about Mandy and her family. Write the questions.

1. _How long are they going to New York for_ ? A week.
2. _____ ? The Plaza.
3. _____ ? They're going to see the Terracotta Army.
4. _____ ? A Jeep.
5. _____ ? Next spring.
6. _____ ? A new house.

Prepositions

11 Adjective + preposition

1 Complete these sentences using *of* or *with*.

1. You must be fed up _____ listening to me complaining about my work—how has your day been?

2. I've always been jealous _____ people who can sing well. Even my cat leaves the room when I start singing.

3. I've put a lot of work into this essay, and I'm really proud _____ it.

4. I thought I was getting a toothache, but the dentist said there's nothing wrong _____ my teeth at all.

2 Complete these sentences using *about* or *for*.

1. I feel really sorry _____ Lucy. First day of her vacation and she has the flu.

2. Are you serious _____ starting your own business? It's a very risky thing to do, you know.

3. We're very excited _____ going to Egypt. We've always wanted to see the pyramids.

4. I think it was Van Gogh who was famous _____ painting sunflowers, wasn't it?

3 Complete these sentences using *in* or *to*.

1. Are you and Jim interested _____ tennis? I think I can get some tickets for the U.S. Open next week.

2. You don't look at all similar _____ Mark. It's difficult to believe he's your brother.

3. Who's that woman over there dressed _____ black? I want someone to introduce me to her.

4. Thank you so much. I'll never forget how kind you've been _____ me.

4 Complete these sentences with the correct preposition.

1. **A** Did you try that new Italian restaurant?

   B Yeah. The food was OK, but I wasn't satisfied _____ the service.

2. It's typical _____ Bob to disappear when it's time to do the dishes!

3. **A** Excuse me, could you tell me where the post office is?

   B I'm sorry, I'm not familiar _____ this area myself.

4. **A** Good morning. *Grantech Solutions.*

   B Hello. I'd like to speak to the person responsible _____ recruitment, please.

Listening

12 Friends of the earth

1 **CD1 19** Listen to three students, Debbie, Jake, and Steve, discussing whether to go to a protest at the local airport. Are these sentences true (✓) or false (✗)? Correct the false ones.

1. The airport already has two runways.
2. Air travel accounts for 15% of carbon dioxide emissions.
3. There is twice as much air travel as there was 15 years ago.
4. The protest will produce its own energy needs.
5. They decide to go to the protest on Tuesday.

2 Complete the lines from the conversation with the correct future form.

1. He _____ (meet) his counselor this afternoon to talk about changing majors.

2. Well, to be honest, I'm not so sure a protest _____ (make) a difference on this one.

3. … you think they _____ (ban) air travel some day soon, do you?

4. I _____ (not get) involved in anything illegal or violent.

5. I don't know if it's legal or illegal, but I'm sure it _____ (be) completely non-violent.

6. I _____ (pick) you both up at 10:00.

CD1 19 Listen again and check.

6 What matters to me

Grammar: Information questions • Adjectives and adverbs
Vocabulary: Antonyms • Phrasal verbs in context
Pronunciation: Word stress

Question forms

1 Matching questions and answers

1 Read the questionnaire. Write questions a–l in the correct place.

> a. How many times have you moved in the past five years?
> b. Who do you live with?
> c. What car do you drive?
> d. Which book has influenced you most?
> e. How long does it take you to get ready in the morning?
> f. How often do you travel abroad?
> g. Whose genes have you inherited, your mother's or your father's?
> h. How much time do you spend on your own?
> i. What objects do you always carry with you?
> j. What music is on your iPod?
> k. What are you afraid of?
> l. What are you like in the morning?

2 Find a question in Exercise 1 with:

- [ ] *how* + adverb
- [ ] *what* + noun
- [ ] *which* + noun
- [ ] *whose* + noun
- [ ] *how much*
- [ ] *how many*
- [ ] a preposition at the end

THE FIVE-MINUTE QUESTIONNAIRE

We talk to the writer Simon Trelawney about his life and career.

1. __b__ My wife and two daughters. We share a two-bedroom apartment but only one bathroom, unfortunately.

2. _____ Just once. We've been here for three years, but we need to move.

3. _____ Credit cards, organ donor card, and photos of the three girls in my life.

4. _____ I like my own company, so as much as I can without being rude.

5. _____ *The Complete Works of Shakespeare.* How did he do it?

6. _____ BB King; the Rolling Stones.

7. _____ Four or five times a year for business and pleasure. Once or twice on vacation—it really depends on what work I'm doing.

8. _____ I get up at 6 A.M. I'm at my busiest and most productive before anyone else gets up.

9. _____ Two minutes. One minute to shave, one minute to throw on jeans and a shirt.

10. _____ I look like my mother, and I have my father's bad temper. It's an unfortunate combination.

11. _____ An ancient second-hand Mercedes.

12. _____ That anything bad might happen to my wife or kids.

Questions

2 Questions with *what / which / whose*

Write a question with *what / which / whose* + noun.

1. Do you want to get up at 6:00? 7:00? 8:00?

   What time do you want to get up?

2. Are you looking for a small shirt? Medium? Large?

   _____

3. Is this Jane's coat? Annie's? Henry's?

   _____

4. Is your wife Brazilian? Spanish? Lebanese?

   _____

5. Do you read *The Times*? *The Post*? *USA Today*?

   _____

6. Do you like classical music? Rock 'n' roll? Jazz?

   _____

7. Did you go to Oxford University? The Sorbonne? Harvard?

   _____

8. Is your phone an Ericsson? A Samsung? A Nokia?

   _____

9. Is it the 39 bus that goes to the station? The 18? Or the 103?

   _____

10. Is this my dictionary or your dictionary?

   _____

11. Is your house number 3? Number 33?

   _____

12. Do you want this one or that one?

   _____

3 Questions with *how*

Write a question with *how* + adjective / adverb.

1. " **How long** is the Panama Canal?"
   "About fifty miles from the Atlantic to the Pacific."

2. "_____ is it from your house to school?'
   "About three miles."

3. "_____ does it take you to get to school?'
   "Forty-five minutes if the traffic is OK."

4. "_____ can your car go?"
   "The top speed is 150 mph."

5. "_____ time do you spend watching TV?"
   "I guess about four hours a day."

6. "_____ times have you been on a plane?"
   "Three."

7. "_____ do you go to the dentist?"
   "Three or four times a year."

8. "_____ have you known your girlfriend?"
   "We were in school together, so all my life."

9. "_____ are you?"
   "I'm 6 feet tall."

10. "_____ did your baby weigh when she was born?"
   "7 pounds 5 ounces."

4 More questions

Match a question in **A** with an answer in **B**.

A
1. **b** What does this button do?
2. ☐ What is this remote control for?
3. ☐ What are your parents like?
4. ☐ How are your parents?
5. ☐ What are tennis rackets made of these days?
6. ☐ You shouted at him? What did you do that for?
7. ☐ How many of you are there?
8. ☐ What did you do to your leg?

B
a. Graphite and titanium.
b. It sets the timer.
c. If you count the kids, there are ten of us.
d. They're fine, thanks.
e. I twisted my ankle playing football.
f. Because he was really annoying me!
g. It controls the stereo system.
h. They're a lot of fun. Not too embarrassing.

5 Questions with a preposition

Complete the questions with a preposition at the end.

1. **A** I think Jamie's in love.
   B Who _is he_ in love _with_?
   A Beth, of course. He's crazy about her.

2. **A** Dad, can I have the car tonight?
   B What _____ want it _____?
   A I'm going out with a couple of friends. Is that OK?

3. **A** There's someone's phone on the table.
   Who _____ belong _____?
   B It's mine. Thanks.

4. **A** Jack's granddad died last week.
   B Oh, no! What _____ die _____?
   A A heart attack.

5. **A** I am REALLY angry.
   B What _____ so angry _____?
   A My bank has charged me $20 for being 50 cents overdrawn.

6. **A** Pierre's the director of a European company.
   B Really? Who _____ work _____?
   A *Allgemeine Union.*

7. **A** We can't go yet! Not everyone's here.
   B Who _____ waiting _____?
   A Anna. She's getting ready.

8. **A** Do you like my new dress?
   B Where _____ get it _____?
   A Beebo's at the mall.

9. **A** Mary got married last weekend.
   B Really! Who _____ get married _____?
   A A guy she met in Japan.

10. **A** I had a great conversation with Joe the other day.
    B Oh, yes? What _____ talk _____?
    A His relationship with his boss. Very interesting.

6 Questions in context

Look at Kathy's profile on her website.
Write the questions.

Kathy Weller

profile

1.	HOMETOWN	Chicago
2.	OCCUPATION	student
3.	STUDYING	Economics
4.	WHERE	Northwestern University
5.	BIRTHDAY	October 18th 1986
6.	RELATIONSHIP	single
7.	LIVES WITH	3 friends
8.	HAIR	blond
9.	EYES	blue
10.	HEIGHT	5'6"
11.	CLOTHES	chic
12.	APPEARANCE	glamorous
13.	CHARACTER	passionate, fun-loving
14.	INTERESTS	movies, sports, going out with friends
15.	MUSIC	R 'n' B, hip-hop

1. Where _does she live_ ?
2. What _does she do_ ?
3. _____ ?
4. Which _____ at?
5. _____ ?
6. _____ going out with anyone?
7. _____ ?
8. _____ ?
9. _____ ?
10. How _____ ?
11. What sort _____ ?
12. _____ look like?
13. _____ like as a person?
14. _____ like doing?
15. What kind _____ ?

Tenses and questions

7 A place of my own

1 Read about Sean's shed. Put the verb forms from the box in the correct place in the text.

made	were bought	estimates
has built	spend	is situated
was given	're learning	were stolen

Sean's secret hide-away

Ever since he was four, Sean Matthews (1) **has been making** things. He's now 14, and this is the third shed that he (2) _____. He even helps his friends with their sheds. "I've always had tools," he says. "I (3) _____ my first tool set when I was five. When I was eight, I (4) _____ bookcases and a desk for my bedroom." Not surprisingly, at school his favorite subject is Design and Technology. "We (5) _____ how bridges are constructed. It's fascinating," says Sean.

His hut (6) _____ in a secluded spot in a field behind his parents' farmhouse. Sean designed and built everything himself. He had no help at all. He laid the stones, nailed the wooden boards, and painted the windows and door blue.

Most of the materials were "borrowed" (which means they (7) _____!) from the renovation of the family home. The shed is made of wood with a tiled roof. The furnishings (8) _____ from thrift stores for next to nothing. Sean (9) _____ that the shed cost a couple of hundred dollars and took three months to build.

"I (10) _____ a lot of time here," he says. "Four or five hours a day. It's great to be able to get away from nagging parents, always telling me what to do. I like to be by myself."

Inside, the hut is cozy and well-equipped. It has running water, a small kitchen, and bunk beds. During the summer months Sean has friends over to stay. They sit outside around a camp fire and look at the stars. "It fills me with a peace that you can't imagine," says Sean.

2 Complete the questions.

1. How long **has he been making things** _____ ? Since he was four.
2. How many _____ ? Three.
3. _____ ? Blue.
4. _____ ? Wood.
5. _____ ? $200.
6. _____ ? Three months.
7. _____ time _____ ? Four or five hours a day.
8. _____ like inside? It's cozy and well-equipped.

Adjectives

8 -ed/-ing adjectives

1 Complete the story about Happy Hannah. Use the words in parentheses. Add -ed or -ing. Sometimes the spelling changes.

Happy Hannah

Happy Hannah thinks her job is
(1) **exciting** (excite) because it's very
varied. It isn't easy, and she has to
work hard, but she likes it, so it's
(2) _____ (reward) as well.

If her clients are (3) _____ (satisfy) with the service they
get from her, Hannah is happy. When she meets her targets, and her boss
tells her she's wonderful, she's (4) _____ (delight), obviously.

Hannah has an apartment with (5) _____ (stun) views over
the city. Her boyfriend, Freddy, who has a (6) _____ (challenge)
job in the city, is (7) _____ (overwhelm) by her beauty and totally
in love with her. She is (8) _____ (amuse) by him because he
tells such funny stories.

2 Complete the story about Depressed Dave. Use the words from
the box below. Add -ed or -ing. Sometimes the spelling changes.

confuse	terrify	worry	annoy	~~disappoint~~	exhaust	impress

Depressed Dave

Depressed Dave is (1) **disappointed**
because he didn't get a pay rise.
He's in a lot of debt, so he's very
(2) _____ about money at
the moment.

On top of all that, he isn't sleeping
well, so he always arrives at work feeling
(3) _____ . As he's new at the job,
there's a lot he doesn't understand. People tell him different information,
he doesn't know what to do, which is very (4) _____ for him.
And to make matters worse, his boss is a bit of a bully, so poor Dave is
(5) _____ of her. She doesn't like Dave, the way he talks, and she
isn't (6) _____ by the way he dresses, either. In fact, she is pretty
(7) _____ by everything about him.

Adverbs

9 Position of adverbs

Adverbs sound better in a certain position.
I often get headaches.
I like modern art very much.

Put the adverbs in the correct place in the
sentence.

1. You'll succeed if you don't work hard.
   (never)

   _____

2. I've finished my homework but not quite.
   (almost)

   _____

3. She's coming to the party. (definitely)

   _____

4. You behaved yesterday. I'm ashamed of you.
   (very badly)

   _____

5. They love each other. (deeply)

   _____

6. I don't like her. (really)

   _____

7. He earns $20,000 a year. (only)

   _____

8. He always wears a sweater, in the summer.
   (even)

   _____

9. The water isn't warm to go swimming.
   (enough)

   _____

10. It's cold for me. (too / much)

    _____

11. I want a cup of coffee. (just)

    _____

12. He wasn't injured. (fortunately, / seriously)

    _____

13. I forgot her birthday. (completely)

    _____

14. I don't like skiing. (at all / very much)

    _____

15. When did you see Peter? (last)

    _____

Vocabulary

10 Antonyms

1 Match an adjective in **A** with its opposite in **B**.

A		B	
1. ☐	hardworking	a.	part-time
2. ☐	old-fashioned	b.	stressful
3. ☐	casual	c.	lazy
4. ☐	good-looking	d.	sharp
5. ☐	full-time	e.	rude
6. ☐	polite	f.	modern
7. ☐	relaxing	g.	unattractive

A		B	
1. ☐	easygoing	a.	stupid
2. ☐	poor	b.	cruel
3. ☐	bad-tempered	c.	calm
4. ☐	second-hand	d.	fussy
5. ☐	smart	e.	modest
6. ☐	kind	f.	well off
7. ☐	big-headed	g.	brand new

2 Complete the sentences with a word from the boxes in Exercise 1.

1. **A** "He isn't very polite, is he?"
   B "No. In fact, he's incredibly _rude_."

2. **A** "They need to modernize the way they work."
   B "True. Some of their business practices are very _____."

3. **A** "Camping is not a relaxing vacation, is it?"
   B "That's true. It's a very _____ way of spending a vacation."

4. **A** "Jane's such a lazy person."
   B "Strange. Her brother is very _____."

5. You can't wear jeans to an interview! You have to look _____!

6. My girlfriend gets angry about everything. She's so _____.

7. George's kids are such _____ eaters. They don't eat bread, or cheese, or anything green. They only eat pasta.

8. **A** "I'm so stupid. I ran out of gas on the highway."
   B "Yeah, that wasn't very _____."

9. Pete's always talking about how much money he has, the fabulous vacations he takes, and how intelligent he is. He's so _____.

10. I know Pete has money, but really he isn't that _____. He owes the bank a lot.

Pronunciation

11 Word stress

1 The unstressed syllables in words are often pronounced as the weak sound /ə/.

This is the most common vowel sound in spoken English.

/ə/	/ə/ /ə/	/ə/ /ə/
global	policeman	performance

CD1 20 Listen and repeat.

2 **CD1 21** Listen to these words. Write in the /ə/ sounds.

/ə/ /ə/		
conversation	politeness	banana
attention	sociable	preparation
apartment	international	customer
personal	intelligent	surprising

CD1 21 Listen again and repeat.

3 Complete the sentences with another form of the word in **bold**. Mark the /ə/ sound in both words.

1. I love his **photographs**. He's definitely my favorite _photographer_.
   (/ə/ over photographs; /ə/ /ə//ə/ over photographer)

2. Dave studied **politics** in college, but he never wanted to become a _____.

3. **Technology** advances so quickly these days. It's impossible to imagine what _____ changes there will be in the next 20 years.

4. Bill doesn't seem to like **vegetables**. I can't understand why he's a _____.

5. The role of **employment** agencies is to help _____ find suitable workers.

6. I know anything's **possible** in soccer, but do you think the U.S. ever winning the World Cup is a real _____?

CD1 22 Listen and check. Repeat the sentences, paying attention to the /ə/ sounds in both words.

Phrasal verbs

12 Phrasal verbs in context (1)

Complete the conversations with a phrasal verb from the box in the correct form. The definitions in parentheses will help you.

Trips
get going   pick up   hold on   get in

A You're arriving in New York next Monday, right?
B Yes, that's right.
A I'll (1) _____ you _____ (come and get) if you like.
B That would be great.
A What time does your train (2) _____ (arrive)?
B (3) _____ (Wait), I'll just check on the ticket. Um…5:45.
A OK. The traffic's bad at that time, but if I (4) _____ (leave the house) at about 5:00 P.M., I'll be there in plenty of time.

Moving
get down to   bring up   work out   settle in

A I hear you just moved. How (5) _____ you _____ (adapt to your new surroundings)?
B Not bad. It's all a little chaotic, so it's hard to (6) _____ (finally start doing) work.
A And the kids?
B Well, we moved to the country because we didn't want to (7) _____ them _____ (educate and care for) in the city. They're finding it tough at the moment. They left their friends behind.
A I'm sure it will all (8) _____ (get better). Give it time.

Relationships
put up with   split up   get over   go out with (someone)

A Did you hear that Sam and Dee have (9) _____ (end a relationship, separate)?
B Really? They've been (10) _____ (be boyfriend and girlfriend) for years! What went wrong?
A Sam said all they did was argue, and he couldn't (11) _____ (tolerate) it anymore. Dee apparently is very upset.
B I'm sure she is, but she'll (12) _____ (begin to feel better) it. He wasn't that great.

Hurry up!
hold up   go on about   calm down   come on

A (13) _____ (hurry up)! We're late!
B All right! There's no need to panic. (14) _____ (become less agitated)!
A Get moving! How long does it take you to get ready?
B There's no need to (15) _____ (talk endlessly in an annoying way) it. I'm moving as fast as I can.
A But we might get (16) _____ (make late) in traffic. Then we'd be really late.

Listening

13 My favorite room

1 **CD1 23** Listen to Dan and Laura talking about their favorite room in their homes. Complete the chart.

	Dan	Laura
Room	attic room	
Size		pretty big
Flooring	wooden, floorboards	
Wall color		a warm shade of blue
Furniture	coffee table, sofa, lamp	
Windows		huge bay window

2 Choose the correct answer.

1. It feels so *good / well* to have more space.
2. … especially when the kids are being *noisy / noisily*.
3. That sounds *wonderful / wonderfully* old-fashioned!
4. … when I want to read, or even to just sit *quiet / quietly* on my own for a while.
5. … blues can be quite cold if you don't choose *careful / carefully*.
6. … if you can't find anything you like in the stores, you have to get *creative / creatively*, don't you?
7. … even in winter, especially in the morning when the sun shines *straight / straightly* into it.
8. I like to wake up *slow / slowly* as I watch the first people setting off for work.

CD1 23 Listen again and check.

7 Fashions and Passions

Grammar: Present Perfect Simple and Continuous – active and passive • Prepositions – noun + preposition
Vocabulary: *be* and *have*
Pronunciation: sentence stress

Present Perfect or Past Simple?

1 Who's who?

1 Match the sentences with the people.

1. **b** He only sold one painting while he was alive.
2. ☐ She married three times. She died when she was 36.
3. ☐ She has adopted three children.
4. ☐ He's been living in Los Angeles for over thirty years. He prefers the light there.
5. ☐ She's written seven Harry Potter books. She's been writing stories since 1971.
6. ☐ She wrote *Pride and Prejudice* when she was in her twenties.
7. ☐ He's had a successful solo career since leaving the boy band, *'N Sync*. He has never been married.
8. ☐ His band was called *The Wailers*. He died of a brain tumor at the age of 36.

2 Complete the questions about the people using the Present Perfect or the Past Simple.

3 Write the answers to the questions in the boxes a–h.

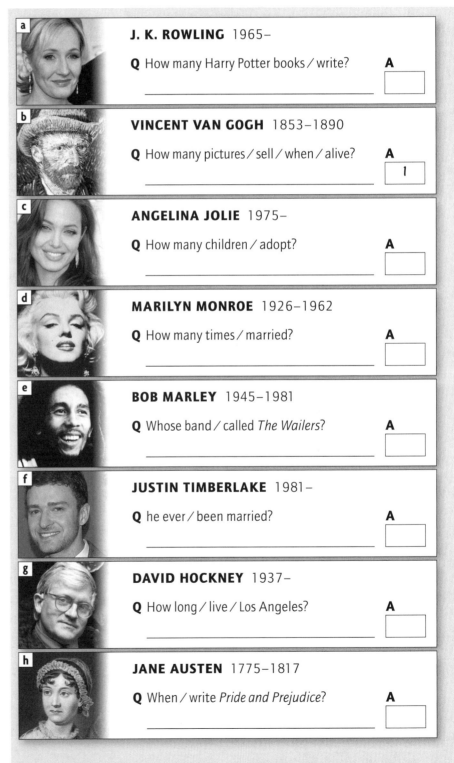

a **J. K. ROWLING** 1965–

Q How many Harry Potter books / write? **A** ☐

b **VINCENT VAN GOGH** 1853–1890

Q How many pictures / sell / when / alive? **A** 1

c **ANGELINA JOLIE** 1975–

Q How many children / adopt? **A** ☐

d **MARILYN MONROE** 1926–1962

Q How many times / married? **A** ☐

e **BOB MARLEY** 1945–1981

Q Whose band / called *The Wailers*? **A** ☐

f **JUSTIN TIMBERLAKE** 1981–

Q he ever / been married? **A** ☐

g **DAVID HOCKNEY** 1937–

Q How long / live / Los Angeles? **A** ☐

h **JANE AUSTEN** 1775–1817

Q When / write *Pride and Prejudice*? **A** ☐

2 Choosing the correct tense

Read more about the life of David Hockney.
Put a check (✓) next to the correct form of the verb.

A Bigger Splash

1 David Hockney _____ in 1937 in Bradford, a town in the north of England.
- ○ born
- ○ is born
- ○ was born

2 He _____ interested in painting and design all his life.
- ○ is
- ○ was
- ○ has been

3 Hockney _____ stage sets and books.
- ○ has also designed
- ○ is also designed
- ○ was also designed

4 He _____ at the Royal College of Art from 1959–62.
- ○ studies
- ○ has studied
- ○ studied

5 He first _____ to the U.S. when he was twenty-five.
- ○ went
- ○ has gone
- ○ has been

6 He _____ to Los Angeles in 1976.
- ○ moved
- ○ has moved
- ○ was moved

7 Over the past forty years, he _____ to most parts of the world.
- ○ has traveled
- ○ travels
- ○ traveled

8 His most famous work is called *A Bigger Splash*. It _____ for $5.4 million in 2006.
- ○ has sold
- ○ has been sold
- ○ was sold

9 An exhibition of his portraits _____ at the National Portrait Gallery in London.
- ○ has recently held
- ○ is recently held
- ○ has recently been held

10 He currently _____ with friends in a villa in the mountains above Los Angeles.
- ○ lives
- ○ has lived
- ○ lived

3 *have been* or *went*?

Complete the sentences with *have been* or *went*.

1. **A** Where's Mom?

   B She _____ to the post office.

2. Where _____ you _____ ? You're home so late!

3. **A** Are you going to the library today?

   B No, I already _____ yesterday.

4. If anyone calls, tell them I _____ to lunch. I'll be back at two.

5. We _____ never _____ to Japan, but we'd like to go.

6. **A** When are you going on vacation?

   B We already _____ . We _____ to Florida.

7. **A** What happened to your neighbors?

   B Didn't I tell you? They _____ to live in the south of France.

4 Time expressions

1 Put the word in parentheses in the correct place in the sentences.

1. I heard about your accident. (just)
2. Have you had breakfast? (yet)
3. I finished my exams. (already)
4. Have you been to Thailand? (ever)
5. I haven't seen that movie. (yet)

2 Rewrite the sentences using *for, since,* and *ago.*

1. I last saw him in 2002.
   a. (for) _____
   b. (since) _____
   c. (ago) _____

2. She went to Korea in April.
   a. (for) _____
   b. (since) _____
   c. (ago) _____

3 Read the situations below. What would you say? Use a time expression from Exercises 1 and 2.

1. You're having a salad in a cafe. You stop eating for a minute and the waiter tries to take your plate away.

   Excuse me! _____. (not finish)

2. You had a cup of coffee. Your sister comes in and offers you another cup.

   No, thanks. _____ (have) one.

3. Tom went out two minutes ago. The phone rings. It's someone for Tom.

   _____. (go out)

4. You rush home to see the World Cup final on TV. You want to know if you've missed the beginning.

   _____? (start)

5. It's 9 P.M. You're watching TV. You finished your homework at 8 P.M. Your mom asks why you're not doing your homework.

   But _____. (finish)

6. You meet an old friend. You can't remember when you last met.

   How long _____? (meet)

Present Perfect passive

5 Active or passive?

Choose the correct verb form.

1. Angela *'s just promoted / 's just been promoted* to area manager of Latin America.

2. I *'ve applied / 've been applied* for a job.

3. How many times *have you injured / have you been injured* playing football?

4. Bob's wife *has just lost / has just been lost* her job.

5. My sister *has passed / has been passed* her final exams.

6. My brother *has given / has been given* tickets to the concert.

7. How much money *have you saved / have you been saved* for your around-the-world trip?

8. A strike *has called / has been called* by the air traffic controllers.

9. They *haven't offered / haven't been offered* more money by the management.

10. The population of our city *has risen / has been risen* to nearly a million.

Present Perfect Continuous

6 Simple or Continuous?

Choose the correct form of the verb.

1. I don't believe it! Somebody has *eaten / been eating* my chocolates! They're nearly all gone!
2. How many cookies have you *eaten / been eating* today?
3. I have never *met / been meeting* a nicer person in my life.
4. How long have you *known / been knowing* Charles and Lisa?
5. He's *written / been writing* a book for nearly a year. It'll be finished soon.
6. He's *written / been writing* a book. I saw it in the bookstore.
7. The children are very quiet. They've *watched / been watching* videos all morning.
8. They've *watched / been watching* five already.

7 Producing Simple or Continuous

Complete the sentences with the correct form of the verb in parentheses, Present Perfect Simple or Continuous.

1. Someone _____ (move) my car keys.
   I _____ (look) for them for hours, but
   I _____ (not find) them yet.
2. I _____ (shop) all morning,
   but I _____ (not buy) anything.
3. That's one of the best jokes I _____ ever
   _____ . (hear)
4. I _____ (listen) to
   you for the past half an hour, but I'm afraid I
   _____ (not understand) a single word.
5. A Are you all right? You look terrible!
   B No, I _____ (work) on the computer for hours, and I have a headache.
6. I _____ (try) to lose weight for months.
   I _____ (lose) five pounds so far.

8 Replying with questions

Complete the questions with either the Present Perfect Simple or Continuous.

1. A Esteban is a singer in a band.
   B *How long has he been singing in the band?*
      How many records has he made?
2. A I'm taking driving lessons.
   B How long _____ ?
      How many _____ ?
3. A Jiri is a teacher.
   B How long _____ ?
      How many schools _____ ?
4. A At last! You said you'd be here hours ago.
   B I'm sorry. How long _____ ?
5. A Anna is getting married to Ian next week.
   B How many _____ to the wedding?
      How long _____ Ian?
6. A What a surprise! I haven't seen you for years.
      What _____ all this time?
   B I've been abroad, actually.
   A Where _____ been?

9 Correcting mistakes

Correct the mistakes in these sentences.

1. How long do you know the teacher?
   _____

2. This is the first time I eat Thai food.
   _____

3. I learn English for four years now.
   _____

4. What have you done last night at around 8 P.M.?
   _____

5. How long you been working here?
   _____

6. The World Cup has won by Brazil five times.
   _____

Tense review

10 A newspaper story

1 Complete the newspaper story with the correct form of the verbs in parentheses.
Use Present Perfect Simple or Continuous, and the Past Simple, the active or passive.

The 22-year weekend break

David Davidson, 79, and his wife, Jean, 70,
(1) <u>have been living</u> (live) in Travelodge hotels for
over 22 years. The couple (2) _____ (spend)
more than $150,000 staying at the hotels even
though they own an apartment. They say it is
cheaper than living in their own home.

The couple's love of motel life began in the 1980s when
they (3) _____ (stay) in a Travelodge while visiting an
elderly aunt. They enjoyed their stay so much that when the
aunt (4) _____ (die), they decided to move in
permanently. However, by 1997, they felt like a change, so they
moved to a newly-built Travelodge, only 15 minutes away. They
(5) _____ (stay) there ever since. They return to
their apartment every two weeks to pick up their mail.

Mr. Davidson, a retired banker, says, "We have everything
we need here, and the staff are like family now." Mrs. Davidson,
who (6) _____ (suffer) from a bone disease
for many years and now uses a wheelchair, said, "Our room
here is on the ground floor, so that's good for me, and we
(7) _____ (bring) lots of framed photos with
us, so it feels like a home away from home. Friends and family
come to visit us here, and we even get birthday cards from the
staff."

The couple, who (8) _____ (marry) since 1953
and have a son also called David, even use Travelodges when they
go on vacation. "We (9) _____ (just return) from
three weeks in Savannah, Georgia. We feel it is the only place
to stay," said Mr. Davidson.

Travelodge's director, Paul Anstey, said: "We are
delighted that the Davidsons (10) _____ (make)
Travelodge their home. To recognize their loyalty, their room
(11) _____ (name) "The Davidsons' Suite," and
a plaque (12) _____ (put up) in their honor in
the reception."

"We just love hotel living."

2 Here are some answers to questions about the
Davidsons. Write the questions.

1. <u>How long have they been living in Travelodge Hotels</u> ?
   22 years.

2. _____ ?
   $150,000.

3. _____ ?
   In the 1980s.

4. _____ ?
   Because they felt like a change.

5. _____ ?
   Once every two weeks.

6. _____ ?
   For many years. She now uses a wheelchair.

7. _____ ?
   Since 1953.

8. _____ ?
   To recognize their loyalty.

Vocabulary

11 *be* and *have*

1 There are many expressions formed with the verbs *be* and *have*. Match *be* and *have* with their expressions

crazy about	about to	a lot in common	fun
a problem (with)	sure of	time off work	into
off (work)	a word with	interested in	
in touch (with)	away on business	a great time	

be	have

2 Read conversations 1–3 and complete them with the correct form of the expressions from Exercise 1.

1. **A** Do you like Jen?
   B Like her! I'm _____ her.
   A I didn't think she was your type.
   B What do you mean? We _____ a great time together. We have a lot _____ .
   A Really?
   B Well, yes. She likes opera and so do I.
   A What? Since when have you been _____ opera?
   B Well, I am now.

2. **A** Can I have _____ with you?
   B What about?
   A Well, you've had a lot of time _____ work lately.
   B I'm sorry.
   A You _____ off four times last month.
   B I know, I've _____ a lot of family problems.
   A What kind of problems?
   B Um—I'd rather not say.

3. **A** I'll miss you.
   B I'll miss you too.
   A You're _____ on business so much.
   B Don't worry. I'll be in _____ as soon as I get there.
   A Look, you have to go. Your flight's _____ to board.
   B Bye. Don't _____ too much fun while I'm away.
   A You can be _____ of that! Bye, _____ a good time!

Prepositions

12 Noun + preposition

Complete the sentences with a preposition from the box.

on (x 3)	to (x 3)	in (x 3)
with	by	between

1. What's the difference _____ *lend* and *borrow*?
2. There's been a big change _____ the weather recently.
3. We need to find a solution _____ this problem.
4. How much do you spend on food every week _____ average?
5. The trouble _____ you is that you don't listen to anybody.
6. I can't get access _____ my Internet bank account at the moment.
7. Tim didn't break your camera _____ purpose. It was an accident!
8. Congratulations _____ your engagement! When's the wedding?
9. Be careful what you say to Adam, he's _____ a bad mood today.
10. There's been a huge increase _____ gun crime recently.
11. I don't think there's really an alternative _____ traveling by air sometimes.
12. There are no rules for prepositions, you just have to learn them _____ heart.

Pronunciation

13 Sentence stress

1 The main stress in a sentence is on the words that give key (important) information.

CD1 24 Listen to the beginning of a conversation in a menswear department.

A	Can I <u>help</u> you?
C	<u>Yes</u>, please. I'm looking for a <u>sweater</u>.
A	What <u>size</u> are you?

CD1 25 We understand the message with just the key words.

A	Help?
C	Yes. Sweater.
A	Size?

2 Read the conversation and <u>underline</u> the words that give key information. (The number in parentheses shows how many words to underline in each line.)

A	Can I help you?	(1)
C	Yes, please. I'm looking for a sweater.	(2)
A	What size are you?	(1)
C	I usually wear a large.	(1)
A	And what color are you looking for?	(1)
C	Some kind of green.	(1)
A	What about this one? Do you like this?	(2)
C	No, I think the style is nice, but it's too bright.	(5)
A	Well what about this one then? It's a much darker green.	(3)
C	Oh, yes, I like that one much better. Is it made of cotton?	(4)
A	Yes, and it's machine-washable.	(3)
C	That's great. Can I try it on?	(3)
A	Of course. The dressing rooms are over there.	(5)

3 **CD1 26** Listen to the conversation. Notice the stress on the key words. Listen and repeat.

Listening

14 Applying for a film degree

1 **CD1 27** Listen to Jenny talking to one of the teachers at the Empire Film School about courses in film-making. Complete the advertisement.

Empire Film School

Are you interested in a Degree in Film-making?

The Empire Film School has places available for students who

▶ have a real (1) _____ for film.

▶ (2) _____ their own films for some time.

▶ (3) _____ of directing.

Our graduates have found work in

▶ *feature films*

▶ (4) _____

▶ *commercials*

▶ (5) _____

The degree includes a class on the use of (6) _____ in film.

There are also places available on our Foundation Program, which provides (7) _____ experience of scriptwriting, (8) _____, camera work, and direction.

Interviews held in (9) _____ and (10) _____.

Apply in writing to the Principal.

2 **CD1 27** Listen again. Are the sentences true (✓) or false (✗)? Correct the false ones.

1. Jenny has been crazy about film since she did her Film Studies program.
2. The counselor thinks qualifications are not the only important things for getting jobs in the film industry.
3. Some recent graduates made a feature film that's won a prize.
4. Jenny used a lot of music in the films she made.
5. She isn't sure which area of film she wants to specialize in in the future.
6. The Foundation Program lasts two months, from May until June.

8 No fear!

Grammar: Verb patterns
Vocabulary: Phrasal verb without a noun
Pronunciation: Weak sounds/ sentence stress

Verb patterns

1 Going to work in Africa

1 Read the conversation between Alan and Betty. Underline the correct verb pattern.

GOING TO WORK IN AFRICA

Alan I'm thinking of (1) *apply / applying* for a job in East Africa, in Tanzania.

Betty Really? I used (2) *living / to live* there.

A I know, I remember you (3) *saying / to say*. I'd like (4) *asking / to ask* you about it, if that's OK.

B Go ahead. I'll do my best (5) *remembering / to remember*. I was there for two years, but that was ten years ago.

A So, what was it like?

B It was a great experience. I liked everything except the climate. I didn't enjoy (6) *working / to work* in the heat.

A Ah, I can't help (7) *worrying / to worry* about the heat. Was it really difficult (8) *keep / to keep* cool?

B Not if you are lucky enough (9) *having / to have* air-conditioning, but we just had fans. And we were on the coast, near Dar es Salaam, and it's really hot and humid there. Where is your job based?

A A town called Arusha.

B Oh, very nice. That's much cooler, inland, near Mt. Kilimanjaro. I'll never forget (10) *climbing / to climb* Kilimanjaro.

A Oh, I'd love (11) *doing / to do* that and go on safari. Did you manage (12) *travel / to travel* around much?

B Oh yes, we went to most of the big game parks—you know, like the Serengeti Plain and the Ngorongoro Crater—that was so huge it made me (13) *feel / to feel* very small, and the wildlife was fantastic. Once, on the Serengeti, a whole family of monkeys decided (14) *playing / to play* on the roof of our car. We didn't dare (15) *moving / move*.

A Which animals did you like best?

B Actually, I think it was the giraffes. I loved (16) *watching / watch* the way they raise their long necks to eat. Oh, and the lions, of course. Do you know that in Lake Manyara National Park the lions actually climb trees?

A Really? It all sounds so exciting. I'm definitely going to apply for the job. It's been great (17) *talk / talking* to you.

B Give me a call, and let me (18) *know / to know* if you go.

2 **CD1 28** Listen and check.

3 Complete this summary of the conversation with the verb in parentheses in the correct form.

Alan is thinking of (1) __applying__ (apply) for a job in Tanzania. He asks Betty (2) _____ (tell) him about it because she used (3) _____ (live) there. She tries (4) _____ (remember) what it was like. She says she found it difficult (5) _____ (work) in the heat, and the problem with (6) _____ (live) on the coast was that it was very hot and humid. However, she really enjoyed (7) _____ (go) on safari and loved (8) _____ (visit) the game parks. She saw lions (9) _____ (sleep) in trees, and once lots of monkeys started (10) _____ (play) on the roof of her car. Betty helped Alan (11) _____ (make) up his mind about the job, and he's decided (12) _____ (apply) for it. He's promised (13) _____ (call) Betty and let her (14) _____ (know) if he gets it.

▶▶ **Verb patterns p. 90**

2 -ing forms

Complete the sentences with the -ing form of the verbs in the box.

walk	give up	~~wonder~~	fix	work
help	wake up	find	watch	live

1. I can't help __wondering__ what life in Africa will be like.
2. _____ too much TV is bad for your eyes.
3. I'll repair your watch for you. I'm good at _____ things.
4. _____ a really good job these days is really difficult.
5. My children are afraid of _____ in the dark, so we keep a light on at night.
6. Did you know that _____ is one of the best forms of exercise?
7. Thank you for _____ me. I really appreciate it.
8. _____ in a big city can be very stressful.
9. _____ sweets is easy. I've done it hundreds of times!
10. I earned a lot of money by _____ overtime.

3 Infinitives with or without *to*

Complete the sentences with the infinitive form of the verbs in the box.

buy	~~pay~~	follow	join	stay
be	carry	learn	hurt	show

1. We can't afford __to pay__ all our monthly bills.
2. It's impossible _____ these instructions.
3. Let me _____ you how to do it.
4. I'm so sorry, I didn't mean _____ your feelings.
5. The teacher made the children _____ after school.
6. I want my children _____ to play a musical instrument.
7. My son persuaded me _____ the latest cell phone.
8. Can you help me _____ this box upstairs?
9. I've invited Mr. Smith _____ us after the meeting.
10. My parents have always encouraged me _____ independent.

4 Which two are possible?

Read the sentences. Which two verbs or phrases can fill the gap?

1. The teacher _____ me to be more careful with my work in the future.

   (a.) told (b.) would like c. hopes

2. I _____ eating fast food when I was in college.

   a. gave up b. couldn't afford c. started

3. She _____ to help me paint the kitchen.

   a. enjoyed b. promised c. offered

4. I _____ going to Mexico next year.

   a. am looking forward to b. would love c. am thinking of

5. My father _____ me to take driving lessons when I was seventeen.

   a. let b. wanted c. allowed

6. I'm _____ to have a big party for my next birthday.

   a. looking forward b. planning c. hoping

7. We _____ to find a parking space in the city center.

   a. tried b. didn't manage c. succeeded

8. I _____ driving in the rush hour.

   a. don't want b. can't stand c. loathe

5 Reporting verbs + infinitive

Complete the lines and rewrite the sentences to mean the same.

1. "Please can you translate this sentence for me?" Maria said to Mark.

   Maria asked **Mark to translate the sentence for her.**

2. "Please, please marry me. I can't live without you," Tom said to Mia.

   Tom begged _____

3. "Don't run around the edge of the swimming pool, or you'll fall in," Mary said to her children.

   Mary warned _____

4. "I won't go to bed!" Bobby said.

   Bobby refused _____

5. "You should talk to your lawyer," Ben said to Bill.

   Ben advised _____

6. "Take that chewing gum out of your mouth immediately!" the teacher said to Harry.

   The teacher ordered _____

6 Using a dictionary

Look at the extract from the *Oxford Wordpower Dictionary*. It shows all the possible verb patterns for the verb *agree*.

agree /əˈgriː/ *verb*

➤ SHARE OPINION **1** [I] **agree (with sb/sth); agree (that ...)** to have the same opinion as sb/sth: *"I think we should talk to the manager about this." "Yes, I agree."* • *I agree with Paul.* • *Do you agree that we should travel by train?* • *I'm afraid I don't agree.* **OPP disagree**

➤ SAY YES **2** [I] **agree (to sth/to do sth)** to say yes to sth: *I asked my boss if I could go home early and she agreed.* • *Alkis has agreed to lend me his car for the weekend.* **OPP refuse**

➤ ARRANGE **3** [I,T] **agree (to do sth); agree (on sth)** to make an arrangement or decide sth with sb: *They agreed to meet the following day.* • *Can we agree on a price?* • *We agreed a price of $500.*

➤ APPROVE OF **4** [I] **agree with sth** to think that sth is right: *I don't agree with experiments on animals.*

➤ BE THE SAME **5** [I] to be the same as sth: *The two accounts of the accident do not agree.*

IDM not agree with sb (used about food) to make sb feel ill

Extract from Oxford Wordpower Dictionary, 3rd edition © Oxford University Press 2006

Read the sentences and check with the extract. Is the verb pattern correct (✓) or incorrect (✗)? Rewrite the incorrect ones.

1. Alan thinks it's too expensive, and I'm agree.

   _____

2. She thinks she's right, but I'm not agree.

   _____

3. I don't agree with you.

   _____

4. All doctors agree that not exercising is bad for your health.

   _____

5. She thought we should go, and I agreed it.

   _____

6. They agreed talking about it again tomorrow.

   _____

7 A dangerous moment

1 Read about Dennis Gibney's dangerous moment. Complete the text with the correct words in the boxes.

SAVED BY AN ELEPHANT!

to accompany	~~training~~	to go	not very easy	let	to see

After (1) __training__ for five years to be a doctor, Dennis Gibney wanted (2) _____ more of the world, so he took a job in a hospital in Kathmandu, the capital city of Nepal. It was hard work, and after a couple of months the hospital (3) _____ him have a few days' vacation. He decided that he'd like (4) _____ into the jungle. This is (5) _____ to do on your own, so he asked a Nepalese guide, Adesh, (6) _____ him.

was hoping	made	carrying	to protect	was about to	meeting

They set off at 6 o'clock one morning, with two elephants (7) _____ their equipment. It was hot and humid, especially as Adesh had (8) _____ Dennis buy special thick shoes and trousers (9) _____ him from snakes. Dennis (10) _____ to see lots of wildlife, particularly tigers, because as a child he had always dreamed of (11) _____ a tiger. His childhood dream (12) _____ come true!

2 Complete the lines of conversation between Adesh and Dennis.

It was afternoon, and Adesh told Dennis not to expect to see any tigers because they usually like to sleep in the heat of the day. However, suddenly, in the distance they saw one. Adesh ordered Dennis to keep very quiet. They crept nearer and found a dying deer, lying in the bushes—the tiger's lunch. They could no longer see the tiger, but somehow they could feel his presence. Dennis didn't dare move or breathe. He looked up and found himself staring into a pair of large yellow eyes. The tiger roared and tried to grab his leg. Adesh managed to pull him away, but they had no real hope of escaping. Then, incredibly, one of the elephants appeared. It ran at the tiger, which turned and fled.

They say elephants never forget, but Dennis and Adesh will certainly never forget that it was an elephant that saved their lives.

a. "Don't expect _____."

b. "Tigers usually _____."

c. "Ssshh! I told you _____."

d. "What's that _____ in the bushes?"

e. "I'm afraid to _____."

f. "Help! The tiger's trying _____."

g. "We have no hope of _____."

h. "The elephant's managed to_____."

Phrasal verbs

8 Phrasal verb without a noun

1 Complete the groups of sentences with the correct form of a phrasal verb from the box.

a. **up** can mean *more*

speak hurry save ~~fill~~	up

1. We're going on a long drive. I'll **fill up** with gas.
2. If we want to have a vacation this year, we'll have to _____ .
3. We're late! If you don't _____, we'll miss the plane.
4. I can't hear you! Can you _____ ?

b. **down** can mean *less*

calm slow go cut	down

1. I want to lose weight, so I've _____ the amount I eat.
2. You're driving much too fast! Please _____ !
3. My temperature was 42°, now it's 39°, so it's _____ .
4. Stop getting so upset about things that don't matter. _____ !

c. **out** can mean *end*

drop die go figure	out

1. I'm trying to _____ how much you owe me.
2. Tim _____ of school because he found it too difficult.
3. The fire _____ because we didn't put enough wood on.
4. Tigers are killed for their skins. They're _____ in the wild.

2 Complete the sentences with the correct form of the phrasal verbs in the box.

hold on	~~go on~~	look out	show off
show up	go off	shop around	check in

1. Don't stop talking! **Go on** ! I'm listening.
2. I thought they weren't coming, then they _____ at 10:00 P.M.
3. I'm looking for a cheap flight, so I'll have to _____ .
4. He's always talking about how wonderful he is. He's always _____ .
5. My alarm _____ too early this morning.
6. _____ ! The glass is going to fall! Oops! Too late.
7. You want his phone number? _____ a second. I'll get it for you.
8. The first thing to do when you arrive at an airport is _____ .

Pronunciation

9 Weak sounds

To get a natural rhythm in English, some "grammatical" words are often unstressed. Look at the examples in the chart.

Auxiliary verbs	is are was were do did has have would can
Articles	a the
Pronouns	he she it we you they that which
Prepositions	at by for from in of on with

When they are unstressed, they are pronounced with a weak form.

> She's from /frəm/ Mexico.
> Are /ər/ you sure?

CD1 29 Listen and repeat.

These words are only stressed when used at the end of a sentence, or for emphasis.

Sentence stress

1 The main stress in a phrase or sentence is on key information. Underline the key words in this phone conversation.

> **Assistant** Hello. Callaflight. Can I help you?
>
> **Customer** Yes, I'm looking for a flight to Tokyo.
>
> **A** When would you like to travel?
>
> **C** I was hoping to travel on Friday, at about 9:00 in the morning.
>
> **A** OK. Do you want to travel from New York?
>
> **C** Yes, please. If you can make it JFK, that would be great.
>
> **A** OK ... I'm looking at a flight that leaves at 9:40. Would that be all right?
>
> **C** That would be fine.
>
> **A** And when were you thinking of returning?
>
> **C** It's just a one-way I need. Can I pay for it now?
>
> **A** Sure. Can you give me your credit card details?
>
> **C** It's a VISA card, number 0494 ...

CD1 30 Listen and check key words.

2 Find the unstressed words in the conversation in Exercise 1, and write a /ə/ symbol above them.

3 Practice reading the conversation aloud. You will only have time to repeat the lines if you say the weak sounds naturally!

Listening

10 Interview with a stuntwoman

1 Carla Simpson is a stuntwoman in the movies. Which of the following activities do you think are a regular part of a stuntwoman's job?

- ✓ falling from high buildings
- ☐ driving ambulances
- ☐ using weapons
- ☐ falling off horses
- ☐ acting
- ☐ fire work
- ☐ hand fighting
- ☐ dressing up
- ☐ climbing trees
- ☐ driving

CD1 31 Listen to the interview with her and check.

2 Answer the questions.
1. Who did the stunts for women in the past?
2. Why are stuntwomen very much in demand these days?
3. Why did Carla's teacher tell her to try stuntwork?
4. What does Carla think is most important in making stunts safe?
5. Why can't they let actors do stunts?
6. What scares Carla the most in life?

3 Complete the lines from the interview with the correct form of the verb in parentheses.

1. ... Carla Simpson, who's succeeded in _____ (become) one of Hollywood's top stuntwomen.

2. But of course we expect women _____ (do) the stunts these days, ...

3. And had you always planned _____ (become) a stuntwoman?

4. ... I remember _____ (climb) trees and _____ (jump) off high walls when I was very young.

5. You often get hurt, even on simple stunts, which is why they can't let the actors _____ (do) them.

CD1 31 Listen again and check.

Vocabulary Crossword 2

Use the clues to complete the crossword. All these words and expressions have appeared in Units 5–8.

ACROSS

1. Scientists are sure we'll _____ life on other planets soon. (8)
5. The mark that stays on your skin after you've cut yourself is a _____ . (4)
9. Andy isn't a real vegetarian—he _____ fish. (4)
11. I love curry—in fact, I like all hot and _____ Indian food. (5)
12. These flowers are gorgeous! Let me find a _____ to put them in. (4)
14. I'll come to the talk on philosophy, but I think it might _____ over my head! (2)
16. Do you wear business or _____ clothes at work? (6)
18. I take these painkillers for any kind of _____ or pain. (4)
19. Mao Zedong came from a very _____ part of China. (6)
21. Does Emma have straight or _____ hair? (5)
23. In Greece you can lie on the beach and visit ancient _____ in the same day. (5)
24. At the end of a successful performance, the audience will _____ . (4)
26. It was supposed to cost $80, but I got a 10% _____ , so I paid $72. (8)
30. A "Would pizza be _____ for dinner?" (2)
    B "Sure, that would be great."
31. I think governments should take stronger action against global warming. But until then, we can each _____ our part. (2)
34. A warranty is a written _____ to replace or repair a product. (9)
35. An elephant's nose is called a _____ . (5)
38. I'm afraid Carol and I just don't see eye _____ eye on most things. (2)
39. If you are unafraid of anything, you are _____ . (8)
40. Harry Potter and the Deathly Hallows _____ out in 2007. (4)
42. Football is called soccer in North America to _____ it from American football. (11)

DOWN

1. A "I'm expecting a baby."
   B "Congratulations! When is it _____ ?" (3)
   A "September."
2. Dan is so excited this week. He _____ off on his around-the-world trip next week. (4)
3. We've spent $150 _____ gas this week! (2)
4. Pam is such a relaxed person—she's really _____ going. (4)
6. I've tried to _____ my phobia of dogs, but I've never had any success. (4)
7. This house is a bit of a ruin, but we're going to _____ it to its original condition. (7)
8. There is always a lot of _____ between teams from the same city. (7)
10. I'd love to have a table in my kitchen, but it would take up too much _____ . (5)
13. Sandra could be a supermodel if she wanted—she's so tall and _____ . (4)
15. "To _____ " means to put a new product on the market. (6)
17. The ad said the views from the hotel would be good—in fact they're absolutely _____ ! (8)
20. It's very, very small—it's absolutely _____ . (4)
22. At 16,500 feet above sea-level you can die from _____ of oxygen. (4)
25. We're going _____ Africa. (2)
27. A _____ is a friendly informal conversation, usually between friends. (4)
28. Busy rich people sometimes employ _____ to look after their children. (7)
29. On your hand you have a thumb, and on your foot you have a big _____ . (3)
31. I have so many _____ and so little money, but I'll have to start paying people back soon. (5)
32. Do you think polar bears will really become _____ during this century? (7)
33. I sleep in a _____ . I'm on top, and my younger sister is underneath. (7)
36. Living to a hundred will _____ the norm within fifty years. (2)
37. Computers are already more powerful than the human _____ . (5)
39. I'll wear anything that _____ me. (4)
41. We eat together _____ a family every evening. (2)

9 It depends how you look at it

Grammar: Conditionals • *should/ could/might have done*
Vocabulary: *make* and *do*
Pronunciation: Linking in connected speech

Conditionals

1 Recognizing conditionals

1 Do the quiz. What kind of friend are you?

2 Find examples of these conditional forms from the quiz to complete the chart.

1. *-if* + Present + Present (x2)
If I promise to do something, I do it.

2. *-if* + Present + *will* (x2)

3. *-if* + Past + *would* (x2)

4. *-if* + Past Perfect + *would have* (x2)

What kind of friend are you?

1. You say to a friend, "I'll give you a call tomorrow." But do you?
   a. Yes. If I promise to do something, I do it.
   b. No. I didn't mean it. It was just a way of saying good-bye.

2. You get a text from a friend. Do you reply immediately?
   a. Yes. If a friend gets in touch with me, I always reply.
   b. It depends. If I have something to say, I'll text back.

3. Your friend has bought a dress which she really likes, but you think it is awful. What do you say?
   a. If she likes it, I'll tell her it looks good. It doesn't matter what I think.
   b. I tell her the truth. That's what friends are for.

4. A friend says to you, "If anyone asks where I was last night, say I was with you." Would you lie for your friend?
   a. If it was really important, I'd lie. But I'd want to know what it was all about.
   b. This sounds like it could be something nasty or illegal. No, I wouldn't.

5. Your friend tells you a secret and makes you swear not to tell anyone. Do you?
   a. Of course not. A promise is a promise.
   b. If it was really juicy, of course I'd tell other people! How could I keep it to myself?

6. Your friend left her cell phone at your house, so you read her messages and found out that she'd been saying horrible things about you. What would you have done?
   a. If she'd left her phone anywhere, I wouldn't have looked at her messages. They're private.
   b. If she hadn't wanted me to read her messages, she wouldn't have left her phone. You can't blame me for being nosy!

2 Types of conditional

Match the lines in the charts to make conditional sentences.

No condition (zero conditionals)

present	+	present
Jenny never says thank you Henry always gets angry Does meat go bad	if	you don't keep it in a fridge? you criticize him. you do something for her.

Possible conditions (first conditional)

will	+	present
I'll help you Things will get better Will you still love me	if	I go gray and get wrinkles? you just wait and are patient. I have time.

Improbable conditions (second conditional)

would	+	past
I wouldn't do that The world would be a happier place What would you do	if	people smiled more. I were you. you saw a fight on the street?

Impossible conditions (third conditional)

would have	+	past perfect
I wouldn't have cooked meat The Lakers would have won Would you have gone to college	if	you hadn't had enough money? you'd told me you were vegetarian. the Knicks hadn't scored in the last minute.

Possible conditions

3 *if + will / might / must / should*

Match a line in **A** with a line in **B**.

A	B
1. ☐ If I'm going to be late,	a. we might go skiing this winter. We'll see.
2. ☐ If Tony calls,	b. I'll give you a call and let you know.
3. ☐ If you don't feel well,	c. you'll have to do some exercise.
4. ☐ If you're ever in Boston,	d. tell him I'm out, and I'll call him later.
5. ☐ If we can afford it,	e. turn everything off and start again.
6. ☐ If you want to stay in shape,	f. you should go to bed and get some rest.
7. ☐ If your computer doesn't work,	g. they won't grow, they'll die.
8. ☐ If you don't water your flowers,	h. you must come and visit me.

Improbable conditions

4 What would you do?

1 Read Social Dilemmas 1–7. Put the verbs in parentheses in the correct form.

> **What would you do if …**
>
> **1.** you _found_ (find) a wallet with $20 in it and no name inside?
>
> **2.** you _____ (find) a wallet with $10,000 in it and the name of a well-known millionaire?
>
> **3.** a friend _____ (cheat) on a school exam and got a better grade than you?
>
> **4.** a work colleague, who was poor, _____ (claim) expenses that you knew were false?
>
> **5.** a teenage girl you know _____ (get) too involved in an online relationship?
>
> **6.** you _____ (take) a photo of a celebrity doing something she shouldn't, and she asked you not to give it to the papers?
>
> **7.** your friend _____ (ask) you to lie to her parents so she could go out with a boy?

2 Read the responses. Put the verbs in parentheses in the correct form.

> **a.** _I'd tell_ (tell) her to stop all contact with him. If she _____ (not be) careful, she _____ (can) get into a lot of trouble.
>
> **b.** I _____ (ignore) it. Everyone fiddles their expenses.
>
> **c.** I _____ (tell) her that I wasn't happy, but if she _____ (be) my best friend, I _____ (lie) for her.
>
> **d.** I _____ (keep) it. It's not that much money. How _____ (can) I find the owner?
>
> **e.** I _____ (get) in touch with a newspaper, and I _____ (sell) the photo for as much as possible. I _____ (not care) what she thought.
>
> **f.** I _____ (not give) it back even if I _____ (know) the owner. He's rich. He _____ (not miss) $10,000. For him, that's nothing.
>
> **g.** I don't know what I _____ (do). I _____ (not like) to tell the teachers, but if they _____ (be) important exams, I _____ (be) really angry.

3 Match the responses to the social dilemmas.

1. **d**   2. ☐   3. ☐   4. ☐   5. ☐   6. ☐   7. ☐

Impossible conditions

5 Life-changing decisions

Read the texts. Write sentences in the third conditional using the prompts.

Laura's life Laura majored in economics at a university in New York. She couldn't find work in New York, so she accepted a job working in a bank in Boston. She went out with a man named Mike, who loved her very much, but she knew he wasn't the man for her. Then she met Bruce, fell in love, got married, and had two kids, Bill and Maddox.

1. If / Laura / not study / economics / not get / job.
   If Laura hadn't studied economics, she wouldn't have gotten the job.

2. If / find / job / New York / not go / Boston.

   _____

3. If / marry / Mike / not meet / Bruce.

   _____

4. If / not marry / Bruce / not have / Bill and Maddox.

   _____

Bob and Betty's life When Bob and Betty's children left home, they decided to move to the city, so they sold their house in the suburbs. They couldn't retire because they didn't have much money. They met another couple, May and Lionel. They all got along so well that they decided to go away together. Usually Bob and Betty visited their relatives when they went on vacation, but with their friends they went to Egypt, which they thought was wonderful.

5. If / children / not leave home / they / stay / in the suburbs.

   _____

6. If / have / more money / retire.

   _____

7. If / not move / the city / not meet May and Lionel.

   _____

8. If / not go / Egypt / they visit / relatives.

   _____

6 Questions and answers

Write questions and answers about what people didn't do!

1. **A** It's a shame. I never went to college.

   B <u>What would you have studied?</u>

   A <u>I'd have studied psychology</u> . (psychology)

2. **A** I didn't travel much in my life. I didn't have the chance.

   B Where _____?

   A _____ . (Africa)

3. **A** I didn't win the lottery, so I didn't buy a new car.

   B What kind _____?

   A _____ . (a Mercedes)

4. **A** I saw Tom Hanks in a restaurant. I wish I'd spoken to him.

   B _____ said to him?

   A _____ told _____ . (he was a great actor)

5. **A** Oof! I'm too full to eat a dessert.

   B _____ had?

   A _____ . (chocolate cake)

6. **A** We had daughters. We never had a son.

   B _____ called him?

   A We _____ . (Robert)

7. **A** I always wanted a large family.

   B How many children _____ liked?

   A _____ . (six)

8. **A** I don't think you should have taken I-95. Big mistake!

   B Which road _____?

   A _____ . (US 301)

should / might / could have done

7 Past possibilities

Complete the sentences with a phrase from the box and the correct form of the verb in parentheses.

could have   should have   shouldn't have   wouldn't have

1. James **could have been** (be) a professional football player, but he broke his leg.

2. You _____ (tell) me the truth. I hate it when people lie to me.

3. They didn't invite me to their wedding, but I _____ (go) even if they had. He's all right, but I don't like her at all.

4. Stop using your cell phone while you're driving. You nearly hit that car! You _____ (kill) us all!

5. Sorry, I've forgotten your address. I _____ (write) it down. What was it again?

6. A present! For me! That's so nice! You _____ (bother), really!

8 Advice about the past

Give advice using *should have* or *shouldn't have*.

1. I told her I thought she was weak and selfish.
   You shouldn't have said that. You know she's very sensitive.

2. I drove past your house last night.
   _____ come in and said hello! I was home.

3. I stole some money from my mother's purse.
   _____ . That's so bad!

4. I'm absolutely broke. I don't have a penny!
   _____ so many clothes. You didn't need them.

5. There's a police car behind me.
   _____ through those red lights. That was really silly.

Pronunciation

9 Linking in connected speech (1)

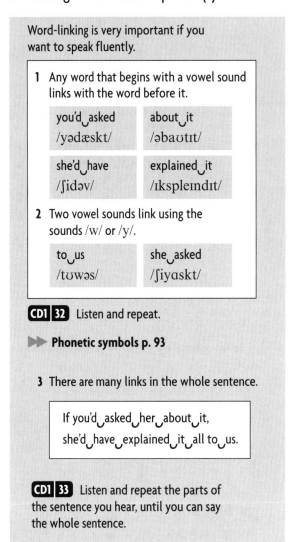

Word-linking is very important if you want to speak fluently.

1 Any word that begins with a vowel sound links with the word before it.

you'd‿asked /yədæskt/	about‿it /əbaʊtɪt/
she'd‿have /ʃidəv/	explained‿it /ɪkspleɪndɪt/

2 Two vowel sounds link using the sounds /w/ or /y/.

to‿us /tʊwəs/	she‿asked /ʃiyɑskt/

CD1 32 Listen and repeat.

▶▶ **Phonetic symbols p. 93**

3 There are many links in the whole sentence.

> If you'd‿asked‿her‿about‿it, she'd‿have‿explained‿it‿all to‿us.

CD1 33 Listen and repeat the parts of the sentence you hear, until you can say the whole sentence.

Read these sentences aloud marking the linking between groups of words.

1. He could have gone home.

2. She might have left early.

3. I should have written it down.

4. We shouldn't have spent all our money.

5. If they'd seen him, they'd have told him.

6. She wouldn't have gotten the job if she hadn't passed her exam.

CD1 34 Listen and check.

Verbs forms for unreal situations

10 What a mistake!

Rewrite the sentences using the words in parentheses.

■ You've got that wrong

A man who robbed a convenience store in Iowa came back to retrieve his wallet, which he'd accidentally left behind. He found the store clerk on the phone describing him to the police and started correcting the facts. "He's about 5ft 10in," the store clerk was saying. "I'm 6ft 2in," the suspect complained. "And about 38 years old," the store clerk continued. "I'm 34," protested the suspect. A deputy sheriff arrived moments later to arrest him.

1. He forgot his wallet. He went back to the store. (if)

   _____

2. He went back to the store. He didn't escape. (if / might)

   _____

3. He started correcting the shopkeeper. (should)

   _____

■ Big bang

Thieves in Kuala Lumpur broke into an office and found the safe, which was holding $50,000. They used dynamite to blow the safe but only succeeded in destroying the whole seven-story building. The safe was left intact. Fortunately, no one was injured.

4. They didn't open the safe. They didn't escape with $50,000. (if)

   _____

5. They used too much dynamite. (should)

   _____

6. It was possible that they killed themselves. (could)

   _____

■ Take me to Detroit

A court in Michigan recently heard evidence from the world's worst hijacker. He was on an internal flight from New York when he leapt to his feet, pulled a gun out of his pocket, fired it twice, and screamed, "Take me to Detroit, or you're all going to die!" When a flight attendant pointed out that the plane was, in fact, going to Detroit, he put his gun away, sat down, and remained silent for the remainder of the flight. He was arrested as he got off the plane.

7. Security officers didn't detect his gun while he was checking in. (should)

   _____

8. He didn't check where the plane was going. He tried to hijack it. (if)

   _____

9. It was possible that he caused the plane to decompress. (could)

   _____

■ A robber with problems

An unfortunate bank robber in Miami had just finished filling his bag with cash when he put his gun in his pocket too hastily and shot himself in the leg. As he staggered towards his getaway car, he tripped on the pavement and knocked out two of his gold teeth. After struggling to his feet, he crossed the road and was run down by a van. Police are looking for a man with a bullet in his leg, two missing teeth, and serious head wounds.

10. It was possible that he killed a passer-by. (could)

    _____

11. He tripped. He knocked out two teeth. (if)

    _____

12. He didn't look where he was going. (should)

    _____

Vocabulary

11 make and do

1 Which expressions go with *make*, and which go with *do*? Write them in the correct columns.

a mistake	up your mind	the shopping
a decision	a mess	someone a favor
sure (that)	the housework	nothing
my best	a speech	a profit
exercises	a noise	a phone call
friends with	the dishes	progress

make	do

2 Complete the sentences using the correct form of the expressions from Exercise 1.

1. First she said yes, then she said no, but in the end she _____ to marry him.

2. I like to stay in shape, so I _____ every day.

3. I love Sundays! I can lie on the sofa all day and _____ .

4. Shh! Don't _____ . The baby's asleep.

5. My teacher says I must work harder, but I can't work any harder, I'm _____ .

6. We have an agreement in our house. I cook dinner every evening, and afterwards James _____ .

7. Could you _____ please? Could you give me a ride to the airport?

8. We have some nice new neighbors. We've already _____ them.

9. Is there a public phone booth near here? I have to _____ .

10. Before you go on vacation you should _____ all the doors and windows are locked.

Listening

12 Scams

1 "Scams" or "cons" are ways of tricking people to get money out of them. Read the leaflet warning people about common scams.

SCAM WATCH!

Watch out for these common scams

1 Your phone rings. When you answer it, the caller checks your name and then tells you that you've won a prize. They ask you to call another number to claim the prize. When you dial the number, they say you will have to pay $50 to get the prize.

2 You receive a fake e-mail, which looks like it's come from your bank, telling you that your security details need to be updated. The e-mail sends you to a website that looks just like your bank's. The website gives you some new security details for your account.

3 A thief steals your credit card without you knowing. He/She then calls you and pretends to be from the police, saying that they've just stopped someone trying to use your card. They ask you for your PIN number.

CD1 35 Listen to Peter and Elaine talking about the scams. Correct any details that are wrong in the leaflet.

2 **CD1 35** Listen again and complete the lines from the conversation.

1. Apparently if you _____ back, the prizes _____ worthless, but they _____ you as much as $50 for the call.

2. Mmm, I must admit, I _____ for that.

3. It's obvious a bank _____ for his PIN number, but you _____ that at the time, _____ you?

4. I mean, if they _____ that one on me now, at least I _____ about it.

5. But honestly, if we _____ not careful, we _____ being suspicious of everyone.

Grammar: Noun phrases • Articles and possessives • *all*/*every*, *myself*/ *each other*
Vocabulary: *a suitcase*/*luggage* • Phrasal verb + noun
Pronunciation: Diphthongs

Noun phrases

1 The $100 laptop

Complete the text about the $100 laptop using noun phrases a–o.

a.	**the** organization**'s** director
b.	**every** child in **the** world
c.	**the** dust and **the** heat
d.	**all** over **the** world
e.	one watt of power
f.	**a** range of
g.	he saw for **himself**
h.	**the** most hard-wearing computer
i.	with **each other**
j.	viewed in bright sunlight
k.	children**'s** lives
l.	**a** big problem
m.	50% of **the** world**'s** population
n.	**a single** battery
o.	**their** own laptop

$100 laptops
for the world's children

Low-cost laptops designed to give (1)☐*b* access to knowledge and education are now in production.

One Laptop Per Child (OLPC), a non-profit making organization, has started mass production of the XO B4 laptop.

Nicholas Negroponte, (2)☐, wants children from (3)☐ to be equipped with the latest technology. It was while he was on a trip to a Cambodian village that (4)☐ how access to the Internet could change (5)☐.

There is no single electricity supply throughout the world, so power is (6)☐. The B4 computer can be powered in several ways, including a pull cord, and a solar panel. It uses less than (7)☐ and can operate for more than 12 hours using (8)☐.

The machine has a 500MHz processor with flash memory instead of a hard drive. It has four USB ports and connects to the Internet through wi-fi technology. It has both a color and monochrome display so that it can be (9)☐. Users will be able to share data (10)☐ easily.

The laptop is more flexible and (11)☐ ever designed. It is engineered to withstand the harsh environmental conditions found in developing countries—from (12)☐ of the Libyan desert to the daily downpours of the Brazilian rainforests.

There is a brightly-colored XO logo on the back. Children can select from (13)☐ colors so they can easily identify (14)☐ in a crowded classroom.

The B4 machine is the first of many cheap laptops which aim to enable (15)☐ to have cheap Internet access by the year 2015.

| 1 💻 → 👤 |
one laptop per child

Indefinite article: *a / an*

2 Saying what something or somebody is

What are these things?

1. an XOB4 _is a computer._
2. Apple Macs and IBMs _are computers._
3. A Boeing 747 _____
4. Jets and gliders _____
5. A Mini Cooper _____
6. BMWs and Toyotas _____
7. A BlackBerry _____
8. Nokias and Sony Ericssons _____

Who were these people?

9. Einstein _was a scientist._
10. Newton and Pasteur _____
11. Van Gogh _____
12. Picasso and Monet _____
13. Charles Dickens _____
14. Proust and Tolstoy _____

Put *a* or *an* into the gaps.

15. My daughter's __an__ actor.
16. I'm _____ optimist.
17. Jane is _____ good painter.
18. Jack's _____ interesting person.
19. When I was _____ child, I was afraid of dogs.
20. Peter's _____ idiot. He knows nothing.

Definite article: *the*

3 You know the one I mean

Complete the sentences with words from the boxes.

the environment	the sky	the beach
the government	the country	the future
the mountains	the weather	

1. We need to protect __the environment__ . We pollute it daily.
2. I used to live in _____ . Now I live in the city.
3. How many stars are there in _____ ?
4. No one can see into _____ . Who knows what will happen?
5. I love taking my kids to _____ . We go paddling and build sandcastles.
6. We go climbing in _____ .
7. She's a federal employee. She works for _____ .
8. People talk about _____ because our climate is fascinating.

the doctor	the post office	the door
the salt	the garden	the radio
the bathroom	the library	

9. That's a nasty cough. You should see __the doctor__ .
10. Pass me _____ . It's next to the pepper.
11. Close _____ . It's freezing in here.
12. I go to _____ once a week. I love books.
13. Let's sit in _____ . It's such a nice day.
14. I'm going to _____ . Do you want me to mail your letters?
15. "Where's Ana?"

    "She's in _____ taking a shower."
16. I don't watch TV much, but I like listening to

    _____ .

the best student	the most delicious
the same	the first

17. Pablo is __the best student__ in the class.
18. I'll have _____ pizza as you—cheese and tomato.
19. This is _____ time I've been in love.
20. That was _____ ice cream I've ever had in my life.

No article

4 Things in general

1 Match a line in **A** with a line in **B**.

A	B
1. ☐ Apples ...	a. is full of vitamins.
2. ☐ Fruit ...	b. doesn't lead to happiness.
3. ☐ Bees ...	c. grow on trees.
4. ☐ Money ...	d. are stronger than women.
5. ☐ Men ...	e. are less mature than girls.
6. ☐ Boys ...	f. make honey.

2 Complete these English proverbs with a noun from the box.

~~beauty~~ love variety time honesty crime

1. __Beauty__ is in the eye of the beholder.
2. _____ is the best policy.
3. All's fair in _____ and war.
4. _____ is the spice of life.
5. _____ doesn't pay.
6. _____ heals all wounds.

3 Complete the sentences with a game or academic subject.

~~psychology~~ biology poker chess

1. James is studying __psychology__ at school.
2. _____ is a game of strategy played on a black and white board.
3. _____ is the study of plants and animals.
4. I love playing _____, but I hate losing money.

5 Article or no article?

Complete the sentences with *the* or nothing (–).

Everyday places

1. I go to __—__ school at 8:00. The school is in _____ center of _____ town.
2. My dad's at _____ work. He teaches _____ children and adults.
3. I'm going _____ home now. I'm tired. I'll be at _____ home tomorrow.
4. Good night. I'm going to _____ bed now. Jane's in _____ bed already.
5. My brother's studying _____ Math at _____ Indiana University. My sister's at _____ University of Illinois.

Place names

6. We're staying at __the__ Pierre Hotel on _____ Fifth Avenue.
7. We can see _____ Central Park, _____ St. Patrick's Cathedral, and _____ Chrysler Building from our room.
8. We're going to eat at _____ Palm Tree Restaurant. We used to go to _____ Giovanni's Restaurant until it closed down.
9. I want to see _____ Bronx Zoo, _____ Guggenheim, and _____ Grand Central Station.
10. Last year we went on vacation to _____ Mediterranean. We met people from _____ Mexico, _____ Japan, and _____ Middle East.

Meals

11. What did you have for __—__ lunch?
12. Where should we have _____ dinner?
13. What time do you want _____ breakfast?

Transportation

14. I usually go to work by __—__ bus, but this morning _____ bus was late, so I missed my meeting.
15. I go everywhere by _____ train. I never travel by _____ plane. _____ last plane I took was in 2003.

Nationalities

16. __The__ French love food, but only French food.
17. _____ Italian people have great style.
18. _____ Mexicans are proud of their heritage.

Possessives

6 *my* and *mine*

1 Complete the chart.

Possessive adjective	Possessive pronoun
my	mine
your	_____
her	_____
_____	his
its	_____
_____	ours
their	_____

2 Complete the sentences with a possessive adjective or a possessive pronoun.

1. Why are you taking __my__ car? What's wrong with _____?

2. Pat and Peter's house is nice, but we prefer __yours__. _____ house is bigger than _____.

3. My sister is always taking _____ clothes without asking me. I never take _____. I wish she'd learn that what's mine is _____ and what's hers is _____.

4. Let me introduce you to Mike. He's an old friend of _____. We were at school together.

5. Tim bakes _____ own bread, and Kim makes _____ own jam.

6. The *TJB Bank* has changed _____ name to the *Allied Friendly*.

7 Apostrophe *'s* and *s'*

Write the apostrophes in the correct place.

1. This is Jack's brother, Tommy.

2. What is your mothers maiden name?

3. Childrens clothes are so expensive.

4. Jenny is my brothers girlfriend.

5. Our neighbors children make a lot of noise.

6. Bill and Sues dog is a retriever.

7. I'm going to Adrianas house tonight.

8. Have you seen yesterdays newspaper?

9. I'm having two weeks vacation.

10. Here is tomorrows weather.

all and *every*

8 Position of *all*

Write the word *all* in the correct place in the sentences.

1. In my family we all like baseball.

2. I've spent day on the computer.

3. I've done my homework.

4. Pedro's invited the whole class to his house—of us!

5. I need is a pair of socks.

6. I've wanted to meet you my life.

7. I like kinds of music from classical to jazz to rock.

9 *all / every / everyone*

Complete the sentences with a word in the box.

all	every	everyone	everything	everywhere

1. The police searched __every__ room. They looked in the garden and the basement. They looked _____.

2. There's nothing wrong with your car. _____ it needs is some gas.

3. It was a great party. _____ had a wonderful time. _____ the food was eaten.

4. Burglars emptied my apartment. They took _____.

5. I believe _____ word he says.

6. It's been raining _____ week.

7. You must tell me _____ about your trip.

8. I've spent _____ penny I have. I mean *had*.

Pronouns

10 *myself / each other*

Complete the sentences with a reflexive pronoun (*myself, yourself*, etc) or *each other*.

1. I hurt __myself__ climbing a tree.

2. You should drive more slowly. You could kill _____ if you aren't careful.

3. My children are too young to look after _____.

4. Bye, kids! I hope you enjoy _____ at the party.

5. How long have you two known _____?

6. My mother and I are very close. We speak to _____ on the phone every day.

7. Selfish people only care about _____.

8. I behaved very badly. I'm ashamed of _____.

Vocabulary

11 a suitcase / luggage

1 Match a count noun in **A** with a non-count noun in **B**.

A count	B uncount
1. ☐ a suitcase	a. fruit
2. ☐ a loaf	b. luggage
3. ☐ a job	c. work
4. ☐ a suggestion	d. advice
5. ☐ an apple	e. travel
6. ☐ a trip	f. bread

2 Are these words countable (C) or non-countable (N)?
1. ☒N☐ news
2. ☐ homework
3. ☐ information
4. ☐ furniture

3 Correct the mistakes in these sentences.

1. Can you give me ~~an~~ *some* information about train times?

2. I'd like a sliced white ~~bread,~~ *loaf* please.

3. How many luggage do you have?

4. The news are always very depressing.

5. He gave me a very good advice.

6. I have a lot of homeworks tonight.

7. I'd like some fruits for breakfast.

8. I'm exhausted. The travel was very long and tiring.

9. She has a very good work in the city.

10. I bought all my furnitures second hand.

4 Choose the correct words.

1. People say that *travel / trip* broadens the mind.
2. Could you give me *an advice / a suggestion*?
3. Don't forget to buy *some bread / some loaf* at the store.
4. I'm looking for *job / work* in marketing.
5. What *a lovely weather / lovely weather* we're having!
6. To get a job you need *experience / experiences*.
7. There *'s too much traffic / are too many traffics* in New York.
8. What's on TV? Do you have *a paper / some paper*?
9. *How many times / How much time* have you been to Seoul?
10. *How many times / How much time* do you spend watching TV?

Pronunciation

12 Diphthongs

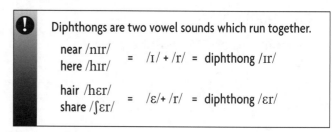

Diphthongs are two vowel sounds which run together.

near /nɪr/ here /hɪr/	=	/ɪ/ + /r/	=	diphthong /ɪr/
hair /hɛr/ share /ʃɛr/	=	/ɛ/ + /r/	=	diphthong /ɛr/

▶▶ **Phonetic symbols p. 93**

1 Write the words from the box next to the correct diphthong.

where	clear	stay	shy	know	sure
now	phone	high	enjoy	poor	deer
aloud	noise	bear	weigh		

1. /ɪr/ = /ɪ/ + /r/   here _____ _____
2. /ɛr/ = /ɛ/ + /r/   hair _____ _____
3. /eɪ/ = /e/ + /ɪ/   pay _____ _____
4. /oʊ/ = /o/ + /ʊ/   go _____ _____
5. /aɪ/ = /a/ + /ɪ/   my _____ _____
6. /ɔɪ/ = /ɔ/ + /ɪ/   boy _____ _____
7. /aʊ/ = /a/ + /ʊ/   how _____ _____
8. /ʊr/ = /ʊ/ + /r/   tour _____ _____

CD1 36 Listen and check.

2 Transcribe the words in the sentences in phonetic script. They are all diphthongs.

1. We caught the /pleɪn/ _____ to the /saʊθ/ _____ of /speɪn/_____ .

2. The /bɔɪ/ _____ in the red /koʊt/ _____ said that he /ɪnˈdʒɔɪd/ _____ the trip.

3. I've /noʊn/ _____ Sue for /ˈnɪrli/ _____ /faɪv/ _____ years.

4. She's /ˈwɛrɪŋ/ _____ a red /roʊz/ _____ in her /hɛr/_____ .

5. Not many people /smoʊk/ _____ /paɪps/ _____ these /deɪz/_____ .

6. He /laɪks/ _____ to /raɪd/ _____ a big black /ˈmoʊtərˌsaɪkl/_____ .

CD1 37 Listen and check.

He likes to ride a big black motorcycle.

Phrasal verbs

13 Phrasal verb + noun (2)

1 Match a phrasal verb in **A** with a noun in **B**.

A	B
1. ☐ apply for	a. a new apartment
2. ☐ run out of	b. a job
3. ☐ clear up	c. an old building
4. ☐ move into	d. your computer
5. ☐ knock down	e. milk
6. ☐ plug in	f. a mess

2 Complete the sentences with the correct form of the phrasal verbs from Exercise 1.

1. We've <u>run</u> <u>out</u> <u>of</u> sugar. I'll buy some at the store.

2. When are you _____ _____ your new house?

3. The kitchen is a disaster! Why can't you _____ _____ your mess after you've been cooking?

4. I _____ _____ a job I saw advertised on the Internet.

5. If your computer stops working, unplug everything, then _____ it _____ again.

6. Did you see? They _____ _____ the old theater to build a new apartment building.

3 Match a phrasal verb in **A** with a noun in **B**.

A	B
1. ☐ sort out	a. an illness
2. ☐ get over	b. a problem
3. ☐ work out	c. the answer
4. ☐ let down	d. your friends
5. ☐ put out	e. the money you owe
6. ☐ pay back	f. a fire

4 Complete the sentences with the correct form of the phrasal verbs from Exercise 3.

1. You promised that you'd help me, and now you won't. You've really _____ me _____ .

2. May I borrow $10? I'll _____ you _____ tomorrow.

3. I've had the flu for about a week, and I'm only just _____ _____ it.

4. "The washing machine's broken, and I'm late for work." "Don't worry. I'll _____ everything _____."

5. The firemen arrived very quickly, but they couldn't _____ _____ the fire, and the house burned down.

6. What's 15% of 2,500? I can't _____ it _____ in my head.

Listening

14 Lost and found

1 Which of these items do you think are most often left behind on public transportation? Number them 1–5.

☐ glasses
☐ bags
☐ coats and jackets
☐ umbrellas
☐ cell phones

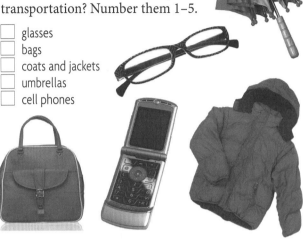

CD1 38 Listen to two colleagues, Mark and Amy, talking about lost property and check.

2 Choose the correct answer.

1. Amy is annoyed about losing her umbrella because it was

   a. new.   **b.** very expensive.   **c.** of high quality.

2. The bags that people most often leave behind on buses and trains are

   a. designer bags.   **b.** shopping bags.   **c.** handbags.

3. At first, people who call their lost cell phones are

   a. rude.   **b.** thieves.   **c.** very grateful.

4. People often leave their laptops

   a. in taxis.
   b. on airport X-ray machines.
   c. in airport departure lounges.

5. Most people who leave their laptops behind

   a. don't realize they've lost them.
   b. don't have time to contact Lost and Found.
   c. think that someone must have stolen them.

3 **CD1 38** Listen again. Complete Amy's description of her umbrella.

> Actually it's a very _____ umbrella
> _____ . It's _____
> — it _____ a golfing umbrella.
> And it _____ down the side of it.

11 Seeing is believing

Grammar: Modal verbs of probability • Continuous infinitive • Prepositions – verb + prepositions
Vocabulary: Word formation
Pronunciation: Linking in connected speech

Modal verbs of probability – present

1 *must / could / might / can't*

1 *Ask Ruth* is a problem page in a magazine. Read Ruth's reply to Luke Basset. What is his problem?

2 Complete the deductions about Luke with the modal verb of probability from the box.

must have (x 2)	~~must be~~	can't have
might not know	may get annoyed	could be jealous
may be studying		

1. Luke **must be** the eldest child in the family.
2. He _____ a younger brother named Cal.
3. Luke's friends _____ with Cal.
4. Luke's parents _____ very demanding jobs.
5. Luke _____ for some exams.
6. The parents _____ that Cal has problems at school.
7. Luke _____ of Cal.
8. Cal _____ many friends.

3 Read about Jane Iverson. What is her problem?

4 (Circle) the correct modal verb of probability in the sentences about Jane and the Fletchers.

1. The Fletchers *must be / can't be* Jane's neighbors.
2. Jane *must have / may have* three sons.
3. The Fletchers *can't be / could be* a retired couple.
4. Jane *must know / might know* about a law.
5. Jane *may be / can't be* thinking of consulting a lawyer.
6. The Fletchers *must have / can't have* children of their own living at home.

Read the original letters on page 88.

Ask Ruth

> Dear Ruth,
> We fight all the time. I hate him! …
> Luke Basset

RUTH SAYS:
Dear Luke,

It is very difficult not to get angry with your brother in your situation. At your age you need time on your own and some privacy when you are with your friends. Ask your parents to find time in their busy lives to sit down and talk to you about what is happening. Tell them how Cal is stopping you from doing your schoolwork. The youngest child in a family is often given special treatment and gets very spoiled. Also, you should tell them about the problems Cal is having at school. He won't leave you alone until he has more friends of his own.

Yours, *Ruth*

> Dear Ruth,
> We live in the house of our dreams.
> We don't want to move but we're going crazy. …
> Jane Iverson

RUTH SAYS:
Dear Jane,

When people live side by side they need to be tolerant of each other's way of life. Your children need their sleep, and you have every right to enjoy your beautiful backyard. Try talking to the Fletchers again, promise that your sons will make less noise during the day if they make less noise in the evenings. Also, you are right, there may be a law controlling the height of garden hedges. However, going to court is expensive. It's in both your interests to sort out the problem yourselves.

Yours, *Ruth*

2 Matching lines

Match a line in **A** with a line in **B**.

A	B
1. ☐ You can't be hungry.	a. They have nothing in common.
2. ☐ She must be out.	b. They've been holding hands all evening.
3. ☐ He can't be American	c. There aren't any lights on in her apartment.
4. ☐ You must be very happy	d. Nobody pays $1,000 for a pair of jeans.
5. ☐ They must be tired.	e. with your excellent exam results.
6. ☐ They must know each other well.	f. We've just had breakfast.
7. ☐ You must be joking!	g. They've been traveling all night.
8. ☐ They can't be getting married!	h. with a name like Heinrich.

3 Why is he late?

1 Mario is always on time for class, but today he is late. Suggest reasons using *must, might, could,* or *may.*

1. Is he still in bed? (might)

   He might still be in bed.

2. Is he sick? (must)

   _____

3. Is he in the coffee shop? (could)

   _____

4. Does he have a doctor's appointment? (might)

   _____

5. Is he stuck in a traffic jam? (may)

   _____

6. Is his bus late? (might)

   _____

7. Is he talking to a friend from another class? (may)

   _____

8. Does he want to miss the test? (must)

   _____

2 Rewrite the sentences in Exercise 1 with *can't.*

1. **He can't be still in bed.**

2. _____

3. _____

4. _____

5. _____

6. _____

7. _____

8. _____

Pronunciation

4 Linking in connected speech (2)

 When *have* is used as an auxiliary verb, it is unstressed. The "h" is not pronounced and the weak form is used /əv/. It is linked with the word before it.

> You should have /ʃʊdəv/ eaten breakfast this morning.

When *have* is a full verb, it is stressed. The "h" is pronounced and the strong form is used /hæv/. It cannot be linked with the word before it.

> You should have /ʃʊd hæv/ breakfast before you leave.

▶▶ **Phonetic symbols p. 93**

CD1 39 Listen and repeat.

Mark the /ə/ sound and the link on *have* in one sentence in each pair. Read the sentences aloud.

1. **a.** He must have won the lottery.

   b. He must have a lot of money.

2. **a.** He might have written it down.

   b. He might have a pen you can borrow.

3. **a.** You should have let me cut your hair!

   b. You should have a proper haircut.

4. **a.** You could have a break soon.

   b. You could have broken something!

Continuous Infinitive

5 Conversations

Complete the conversations with a suitable verb in the Continuous Infinitive.

1. **A** Do you know where Ben is?
   B I'm not sure. He may ___be playing___ games on the computer.

2. **A** Where's Maho?
   B She's upstairs. She must _____ to music in her room.
   A She's not in her room.
   B Try the bathroom. She might _____ a shower.

3. **A** I can't find the thing that changes the TV channel.
   B The remote control? Stand up. You could _____ on it.

4. **A** Have you seen the newspaper?
   B I think James may _____ it.

5. **A** What's that noise?
   B It sounds like an ambulance. It must _____ someone to the hospital.

6. **A** Look over there! It's Mariana and Alex.
   B She can't _____ his hand. She doesn't like him.
   A They must _____ out together. I don't believe it!

7. **A** What's happening outside?
   B It sounds like workers. They must _____ up the road outside.
   A What for?
   B I don't know. They could _____ a broken water pipe.

CD1 40 Listen and check.

Modal verbs of probability – past

6 *must have / might have / may have / can't have*

Look at the pictures. Make deductions about what has probably happened. Write sentences.

- must / accident
- might / snowboarding

_____
_____

- must / argument
- can't / enjoy / meal

_____
_____

- can't / driving test
- may / nervous

_____
_____

4

- could / eat / bird
- bird / might / escape

_____

_____

5

- must / miss / plane
- plane / could / delayed

_____

_____

6

- can't / enjoy / movie
- must / boring

_____

_____

7

- must / cell phone
- might / stolen

_____

_____

8

- must / receive / good news
- may / lottery

_____

_____

7 Rewriting sentences

Rewrite these sentences using the modal verb in brackets.

1. I'm sure they've arrived. I can hear a car. (must)
   They must have arrived. I can hear a car.

2. I'm sure you didn't study hard for your exams. (couldn't)

   _____

3. Perhaps I left my cell in the Internet cafe. (might)

   _____

4. He has probably been on a diet. (must)

   _____

5. It's possible that they got married in secret. (could)

   _____

6. Perhaps he called while we were out. (may)

   _____

Tense review

8 It's hard to believe

1 Read the first newspaper article. Answer the questions.

1. How did Jan lose consciousness?
2. How was Gertruda rewarded for her care and love?
3. How had the world changed when Jan awoke?

2 Here are some sentences about Jan and Gertruda's story. Rewrite them using the words in parentheses.

1. It sounds like it was a terrible accident. (must)

   It must have been a terrible accident.

2. Perhaps Jan had worked for the railway for many years. (might)

   _____

3. Gertruda was probably amazed when he opened his eyes. (must)

   _____

4. I think the doctors didn't expect Jan to wake up. (may)

   _____

5. I don't think Jan had ever seen a cell phone before. (couldn't)

   _____

6. I'm sure they are really enjoying life together now. (must)

   _____

3 Read the second newspaper article on page 75. Answer the questions.

1. What was Arnie doing when he disappeared?
2. When did the family get Lucky?
3. What was Arnie like when he returned?

4 Here are some sentences about Arnie's story. Rewrite them using the words in parentheses.

1. Perhaps Arnie was stolen by a dog breeder. (might)

   _____

2. Arnie is probably a pedigree dog. (could)

   _____

3. I don't think the family expected Arnie to return. (couldn't)

   _____

4. I'm sure the family were surprised to hear from the neighbor. (must)

   _____

5. Lucky is possibly a mixed-breed dog. (may)

   _____

6. Arnie was undoubtedly treated very badly. (must)

   _____

Man wakes up after being in a coma for 19 years

A man has woken up after being in a coma for 19 years to find that his world had changed beyond all recognition.

Railway worker Jan Grzebski lost consciousness nearly 20 years ago after being struck by a train. Last Sunday he opened his eyes to see his devoted wife, Gertruda, looking at him. She had cared for him all through his coma.

She fed and washed him every day and moved him every hour to prevent bedsores. Jan's doctor said, "She has done the job of an entire intensive care team."

Her devotion was rewarded when, at 65 years of age, Jan came out of his coma. But he woke up to an entirely different world from the one he remembered.

"When I went into a coma there were not that many choices," Jan said. "Now I see people on the streets with cell phones, and there are so many goods in stores." He is amazed at all he sees, and says, "The world has changed so much!"

The wife who never gave up on him said she cried and prayed a lot during the long and lonely coma years. She says, "This is my reward for all the care and love."

_____

Arnie the terrier finds his way home after two years

A Tibetan terrier named Arnie, who was missing for nearly two years, has made his way home to his delighted family.

Eleven-year-old Arnie disappeared from his home 21 months ago. His owner, Gillian Singleton, believes he was probably stolen for breeding purposes. "One minute he was playing in the backyard, the next minute he was gone."

Her children David, 9, and Emily, 6, were very upset. The family immediately began a full-scale search for him, but he was nowhere to be found.

As the months passed, they thought Arnie had gone forever. They took in a stray dog, named Lucky, and cared for him.

Then, while the family were on vacation, they got a call from a neighbor saying a dog that looked like Arnie was sitting outside their house! It was Arnie, he had returned after nearly two years. The family were delighted, but poor Arnie was in bad shape and had lost a lot of weight.

Arnie is now fit and well and has been introduced to Lucky. The two of them are getting along really well.

Vocabulary

9 Word formation – adjectives to nouns

1 Make nouns from the adjectives in the box using the suffixes to complete the chart.

ill	curious	conscious	free	disappointed
lazy	bored	stupid	strong	exciting
long	wise	moody	generous	

illness	-ness
	-ment
	-dom
	-ity
	-th

2 Complete the sentences using the nouns from Exercise 1.

1. Jan regained **consciousness** after 21 years in a coma, but it'll be a long time before he has the _s_____ to walk again.

2. He died peacefully after a long _i_____ .

3. In a democratic country _f_____ of speech is very important.

4. Look at the fabulous present Ricardo gave me. I can't believe his _g_____ !

5. I've measured the height, width, and _l_____ of the box, and it fits.

6. His advice is always so good. I really appreciate the _w_____ of his words.

7. She can't get over the _d_____ of not getting that job in the bank, but I can't get over the _s_____ of going for the interview in torn jeans.

8. Karen's difficult to live with because of her _m_____ . You never know if she's going to be cheerful or bad-tempered.

9. Don't keep asking questions. You know what they say: "_C_____ killed the cat."

10. You say everything's boring, and you never want to do anything or go anywhere. Your problem is _l_____ not _b_____ . I want some _e_____ in my life!

Prepositions

10 Verb + preposition

1 Complete the sentences with the prepositions in the box.

for (x 4)	on (x 5)	with (x 3)	to (x 2)
of	from	in	about

1. **A** Why are you arguing _with_ the children _____ pocket money again?

   B Well, they spend their money _____ such stupid things.

   A I know, but you have to see it as money that belongs _____ them.

2. Excuse me, this pen doesn't work. Can I exchange it _____ another one?

3. So you're an architect. What are you working _____ at the moment?

4. **A** We fell in love _____ this house as soon as we saw it.

   B I'm not surprised. I've always dreamed _____ having a living room as big as this.

5. I don't believe _____ astrology—not the nonsense they write in the newspapers, anyway.

6. **A** How did Gary react _____ your suggestion?

   B He wasn't excited about the idea.

7. I'm really busy right now—could you deal _____ this enquiry?

8. The train arriving _____ platform 2 is the 5:27 service to Boston. We apologize _____ the late arrival of this train.

9. **A** Excuse me, we didn't ask _____ salad with our pizza.

   B It comes free with every pizza. You don't have to pay _____ it.

10. This CD I borrowed _____ Anna is great!

11. I like Martin. I can always rely _____ him to cheer me up when I'm feeling down.

12. I told Barbara that I could easily get the bus home, but she insisted _____ giving me a ride.

Listening

11 Shaksper?

1 Do you think these statements about William Shakespeare are true (✓) or false (✗)?

1. ☐ There's no evidence that he was a writer.
2. ☐ He was a businessman.
3. ☐ He was from an aristocratic background.
4. ☐ He went to college.
5. ☐ His daughters couldn't read or write.

CD1 41 Listen to the conversation between Jake and his dad and check. Correct the false sentences.

2 Answer the questions.

1. How did Shakespeare spell his name?
2. How much of Shakespeare's background is in the plays?
3. Who was Edward De Vere?
4. Why does his background suggest that he may have written the plays?
5. How many plays were published in De Vere's name?

3 **CD1 41** Listen again and complete the lines from the conversation.

1. … about how he _____ actually written the plays.

2. Well, I think there've always been theories that Shakespeare _____ them.

3. He _____ even worse at spelling than I am.

4. There's so much knowledge in them—well, you _____ that, …

5. But _____ all that information himself?

6. So, who do these people think _____ the plays then?

12 Telling it like it is

Grammar: Reported speech • Phrasal verbs in context
Vocabulary: Ways of talking
Pronunciation: Ways of pronouncing *ou*

Reported speech

1 Reported speech to direct speech

Read the first part of the newspaper article. Look at the lines in *italics*. Write what Christine Small actually says.

1. "<u> Felix belongs to me </u>."
2. "_____ with my address."
3. "_____ a breeder in 2005."
4. "_____ more of a member of the family than a pet."
5. "_____ for days on end."
6. "When he comes home, he _____."
7. "Paul Flashman _____."
8. "_____ of his own."
9. "_____ terribly."
10. "_____ to get him back."

CD1 42 Listen and check.

2 Direct speech to reported speech

Read the rest of the article. Report the lines in *italics*.

1. <u>Mr. Flashman said that Felix didn't belong to Mrs. Small.</u>
2. He said that the cat _____ _____.
3. He told reporters that _____ his.
4. He claimed that Mrs. Small _____ _____ complete lies.
5. He insisted that Mrs. Small _____ _____.
6. He explained that _____ _____.
7. He thought that _____ _____ because she didn't like him.
8. The police said they _____ _____ the situation.

Fighting like cat and dog

Two neighbors are fighting a legal battle over who owns Felix, a seven-year-old male tabby cat.

The battle began last month after Felix disappeared from the home of Christine Small. She said that (1) *Felix belonged to her* and (2) *he had a collar with her address.* She explained that (3) *she had bought the cat from a breeder in 2005,* and (4) *Felix was "more of a member of the family than a pet."*

She told the police that (5) *Felix had been disappearing for days on end,* and (6) *when he came home, he was not eating his food.* She claims that her neighbor, (7) *Paul Flashman, was feeding Felix,* because (8) *he had always wanted a cat of his own.* She said that (9) *she missed her cat terribly* and (10) *would do anything to get him back.*

Mrs. Small at home with Felix

Mr. Flashman said, (1) *"Felix doesn't belong to Mrs. Small.* (2) *He's been running wild for years."* Mr. Flashman has lived in the area for twenty years, and is a respected member of the community. He told reporters yesterday, (3) *"Felix is mine.* (4) *Mrs. Small told the police complete lies.* (5) *She has never loved Felix like I do."*

He said, (6) *"I have always had a good relationship with my other neighbors.* (7) *I think that Mrs. Small is complaining because she doesn't like me."*

A police spokesman said, (8) *"We will investigate the situation and try to resolve it."*

3 Reporting words and thoughts

1 Report the statements.

1. "I'll miss you very much," he said to her.
   He told her he would miss her very much.

2. "I'm going to Taiwan soon."
   She said _____.

3. "This movie will be interesting."
   I thought _____.

4. "I can't help you because I have too much to do."
   She said _____.

5. "Daniel has bought the tickets."
   I was told _____.

6. "It's a stupid idea, and it won't work."
   She thought _____.

7. "We had terrible weather on our trip."
   He complained _____.

8. "We've never been to Peru," they said to me.
   They told _____.

9. "But we want to go some day," they said.
   They added that _____.

2 Report the questions.

1. "What are you doing?"
   She asked me what I was doing.

2. "Do you want to go for a walk?"
   She asked me if I wanted to go for a walk.

3. "Why are you crying?" he asked her.
   He wondered _____.

4. "Can I borrow your car?"
   He asked me _____.

5. "Where have you come from?"
   The customs officer asked me _____.

6. "How long are you going to be at the gym?"
   She wanted to know _____.

7. "Will you be back early?"
   She asked us _____.

8. "When do you have to go to work?"
   She asked me _____.

9. "How much does it cost to fly to New York?"
   She wanted to know _____.

4 Interview with a bank manager

1 Write the bank manager's questions.

A Come and sit down, Mr. Smith. Now, you want to borrow some money. (1) **How much do you want to borrow?**

B Five thousand dollars.

A (2) _____?

B Because I want to buy a car.

A I see. Could you give me some personal details?
(3) _____?

B I'm a graphic designer.

A And (4) _____?

B Sixty thousand dollars a year.

A (5) _____?

B Yes, I am. I've been married for six years.

A (6) _____?

B Yes, we have two children.

A I see you live in an apartment. (7) _____
_____?

B We've lived there for three years.

A Well, that seems fine. I don't think there'll be any
problems. (8) _____?

B I'd like it as soon as possible, actually.

A All right. Let's see what we can do.

CD1 43 Listen and check.

2 Report the bank manager's questions.

1. First, she asked Mr. Smith <u>how much he wanted to borrow</u> .
2. Then she wanted to know _____
   _____ .
3. She needed to know _____ .
4. He had to tell her _____ .
5. Then she asked _____ .
6. For some reason, she wanted to know _____
   _____ .
7. She asked him _____ .
8. Finally, she wondered _____ .

Reporting verbs

5 Verb + infinitive

Rewrite the sentences in reported speech. Use the verbs in the box.

persuade	order	ask	~~advise~~	tell
encourage	invite	beg	remind	

1. "If I were you, I'd go to California," he said to me.
   He advised me to go to California.
2. "Could you cook dinner?" he asked Sue.
   _____
3. "Hand in your homework on Monday," the teacher told the class.
   _____
4. "Don't forget to mail the letter," my wife said to me.
   _____
5. "Come over and have dinner with us," Marta said to Paul.
   _____
6. "You must pay a fine of two hundred dollars," the judge said to Stanley Fox.
   _____
7. "Buy the black shoes, not the brown ones," Flora said. "They're much, much nicer."
   "OK," said Emily.
   _____
8. "You should sing professionally," Marco said to Anthony. "You're really good at it."
   _____
9. "Please, please don't tell my father," she said to me.
   _____

6 ask and tell

> ❗ Remember that *ask* can be used to report questions and commands, and *tell* can be used to report statements and commands, but the form is different.
>
> **Questions**
> *She asked me where I lived.*
> *She asked me if I wanted a ride.*
>
> **Statements**
> *He told me he was very unhappy.*
> *He told his wife that he loved her.*
>
> **Commands**
> *He asked me to turn the music down.*
> *She told him to go away.*
>
> Notice the negative command.
> *They asked me not to tell anyone.*
> *She told her son not to worry.*

Rewrite the questions, statements, and commands in reported speech using *ask* or *tell*.

1. "Leave me alone!" she said to him.
   She told him to leave her alone.
2. "Please don't go," he asked her.
   _____
3. "I'm going to bed now," he said to Debra.
   _____
4. "How much do you earn, Dad?" asked Jeremy.
   _____
5. "Turn to page 34," the teacher said to the class.
   _____
6. "Can you call back later, Miss Fulton?" asked the secretary.
   _____
7. "You did very well on the test," said the teacher.
   _____
8. "Don't run across the road!" the police officer told the children.
   _____
9. "Are you going to the concert?" Pam asked Roy.
   _____
10. "It's time to get up!" Harry said to his daughters.
    _____

Vocabulary

7 Ways of speaking

Complete the conversation with the correct form of the verbs in the box.

say	tell	explain	speak	talk	reply	ask

I was walking in the park the other day when I met old Mr. Brown, so we stopped and (1) __talked__ for a while. He (2) _____ me that his wife, Jenny, had been taken into the hospital. I (3) _____ him how Jenny was, and he (4) _____ that she was getting better. I (5) _____ Mr. Brown to give Jenny my regards. He wondered why I hadn't been to the tennis club recently, so I (6) _____ that I'd been very busy and just hadn't had time.

"There's something you must (7) _____ me," Mr. Brown suddenly said. "How many languages does your son (8) _____ ?"

"Four," I (9) _____. "Why (10) _____ you _____ ?"

"Well, I know your son has some very funny stories to (11) _____ about his trips abroad and his language learning. We're having a meeting of the Travelers' Club next week, and I'd like him to come along and (12) _____ to us."

I (13) _____ that I would (14) _____ to my son about it, and I promised to get back in touch with him.

Then we (15) _____ good-bye and went our separate ways.

8 Other reporting verbs

Rewrite the sentences in reported speech using the verbs in the boxes. Use each verb once.

complain admit deny suggest explain	that

refuse offer agree promise	to do

1. "I think it would be a very good idea for you to go to bed," the doctor said to Paul.
   The doctor suggested that Paul go to bed.

2. "Yes, OK. I'll lend you $25," Jo said to Matt.
   _____
   _____

3. "Yes, it was me. I broke your camera," said Harry.
   _____
   _____

4. "I didn't pull her hair," said Timmy.
   _____
   _____

5. "I didn't do the homework because I was sick," said the student.
   _____
   _____

6. "If you clean your room, I'll buy you a pizza!" said Jessica's dad.
   _____
   _____

7. "Excuse me! There's a fly in my salad," said Patrick.
   _____
   _____

8. "I'm sorry. I can't marry you because I don't love you," Sarah said to Jento.
   _____
   _____

9. "I'll cook dinner if you like," Amanda said to Kai.
   _____
   _____

Phrasal verbs

9 Phrasal verbs in context (2)

Complete the conversations with the correct form of phrasal verb from the boxes.
The definition in parentheses will help you.

1. A break-in

break into	show up	get by	get away	go off

A Someone _broke into_ (enter by force) my apartment last night.

B Oh, no! What was stolen? Did they _____ (escape) with much?

A Television, stereo, and my laptop. I don't know how I'm going to _____ (manage to survive) without my laptop.

B Did anyone see or hear anything?

A The alarm _____ (start ringing), but that didn't stop them.

B Did you call the police?

A Yes. They _____ (arrive) about an hour later, but there was nothing really they could do.

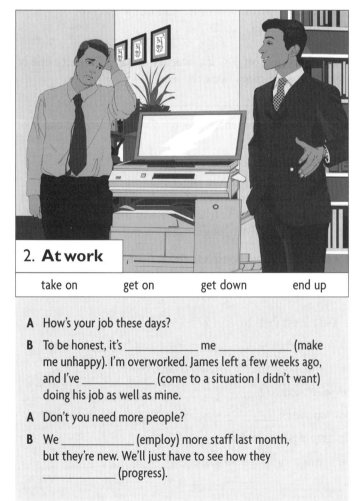

2. At work

take on	get on	get down	end up

A How's your job these days?

B To be honest, it's _____ me _____ (make me unhappy). I'm overworked. James left a few weeks ago, and I've _____ (come to a situation I didn't want) doing his job as well as mine.

A Don't you need more people?

B We _____ (employ) more staff last month, but they're new. We'll just have to see how they _____ (progress).

3. Settling in

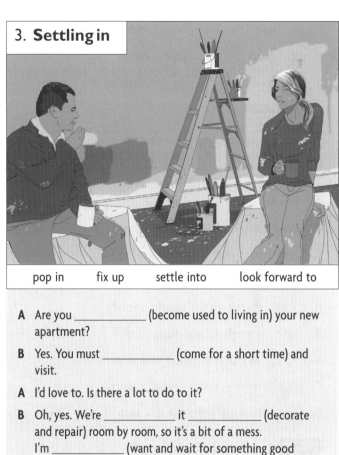

pop in	fix up	settle into	look forward to

A Are you _____ (become used to living in) your new apartment?

B Yes. You must _____ (come for a short time) and visit.

A I'd love to. Is there a lot to do to it?

B Oh, yes. We're _____ it _____ (decorate and repair) room by room, so it's a bit of a mess. I'm _____ (want and wait for something good to happen) the time when it's all finished!

A Be patient! You'll get there.

4. Bad luck

run over	beat up	give up	go on

A I'm having a lot of bad luck right now.

B Why? What's _____ (happen)?

A My sister was _____ (hit by a car) outside her house the other day.

B Oh, no! Is she OK?

A Yes, fortunately. But then my brother was _____ (attack and badly hurt) by someone who tried to mug him. He had to go to the hospital.

B How is he now?

A Well, he's _____ (stop doing) his job for the time being. He'll go back to work when he feels better.

Pronunciation

10 Ways of pronouncing *ou*

CD1 44 The letters *ou* are pronounced in many different ways. For example:

/ɔr/	four	/aʊ/	doubt
/u/	group	/oʊ/	though
/ʌ/	country	/ɪ/	delicious
/ʊ/	would		

▶▶ **Phonetic symbols p. 93**

1 <u>Underline</u> the word with the different pronunciation.

1. /ʊ/   would   should   shoulder   could

2. /ɔr/   your   sour   court   pour

3. /aʊ/   accountant   country   count   fountain

4. /ɔ/   though   ought   bought   thought

5. /ʌ/   enough   tough   rough   cough

6. /ə/   anonymous   mouse   enormous   furious

7. /ʌ/   trouble   double   doubt   country

8. /u/   through   group   though   soup

CD1 45 Listen and check.

2 Transcribe the words in phonetic script.

1. It's the /θɔt/_____ that /kaʊnts/_____ .

2. There's an /ɪˈnɔrməs/_____ /maʊs/_____ in the kitchen.

3. I have no /daʊt/_____ that my boss will be /ˈfyʊriəs/_____ .

4. You /ɔt/_____ to do something about that /kɔf/_____ .

5. I have a lot of /ˈtrʌbl/_____ with noisy /ˈneɪbərz/ _____ .

CD1 46 Listen and check.

Listening

11 *You weren't listening!*

1 Complete these statements as reported speech.

1. "We've run out of brown rice."
    I told you _____

2. "I'll record it for you whenever you're not here."
    You said _____

3. "We had a really awful time in Boston last weekend."
    My sister told me today that _____

4. "I went to Washington, DC last weekend, and I think it's one of the most beautiful cities I've ever seen."
    Lisa said that _____

CD1 47 Listen to an argument between Julia and Colin and check.

2 Answer the questions.

1. Why was Colin so long at the supermarket?
2. Why does Julia want brown rice?
3. Why should they book the train tickets soon?
4. What's happening in Washington, DC soon?

3 **CD1 47** Listen again and complete the statements.

> **Julia** Did you get some brown rice?
>
> **Colin** You didn't (1) _____ brown rice.
>
> **Colin** I never heard you say anything about brown rice.
>
> **Julia** You obviously (2) _____
>
> **Colin** You said (3) _____ last week.
>
> **Colin** Lots of people told (4) _____
>
> **Colin** I think it said in the newspaper (5) _____ .

Vocabulary Crossword 3

Use the clues to complete the crossword. All these words and expressions have appeared in Units 9–12.

ACROSS

3. 50% of young British people have a web _____ on Facebook. (4)
5. If a child lives with _____, he learns to feel worthless. (9)
9. You can't have your chocolate dessert until you _____ up all your spinach. (3)
10. I just watched my team win 6-0. I'm over the _____ ! (4)
13. There was so much traffic, we were _____ a complete standstill for 45 minutes. (2)
14. A doctor will first _____ your illness and then prescribe some medicine. (8)
15. I offered to help Alan but he _____ me to go away! (4)
16. I have a job interview tomorrow. _____ your fingers for me! (5)
20. In most countries you can read and write anything on the Internet—there's no _____. (10)
21. An _____ is where you sell something to the person who offers the highest price. (7)
22. To _____ honest Jane, I'm not too crazy about your hair that color. (2)
23. I've _____ up with a great new idea for a video game! (4)
25. The title above a story or article in a newspaper is the _____. (8)
28. This part of town used to be very unpopular. Now it's a _____ district filled with busy cafes and restaurants. (8)
29. "Ouch! That hurts!"
    "Jane, I thought women have a higher _____ threshold than men." (4)
31. I'm _____ up with waiting at airports. I'm going to travel by train next time! (3)
32. Billy ran away because he didn't feel _____. (9)

DOWN

1. Another word for shocked is _____. (7)
2. Elvis is known _____ "The King." (2)
4. It's so bright outside, I can't read my book. I need some sun _____. (7)
6. If you threw $30,000 into the air in my town center, it would certainly start a _____! (4)
7. What's the expiration date on your _____ card? (6)
8. Could you spare _____ a minute? I need some help with this crossword. (2)
10. Michelangelo's David is considered to be a _____. (11)
11. Nowadays many people don't use a teapot to make tea, just a tea _____ in a cup. (3)
12. A situation where there are no rules, order, or government is described as _____. (7)
17. "It must be true that bats are blind."
    "Perhaps, but I'm not _____ sure." (2)
18. I've always hated that office building—I wish they'd _____ it down and build something better. (5)
19. A _____ is the reason why somebody commits a crime. (6)
20. Jimmy Wales and Larry Sanger both _____ to have created Wikipedia. (5)
22. A piece of paper money, like £10 or $50. (8)
24. "How much does a doctor _____ ?"
    "About $100,000 a year, I think." (4)
25. Fantastic! Our new website is getting over 1,000 _____ a day! (4)
26. The police can only _____ you if they think you are guilty of a crime. (6)
27. Do you have something I can _____ for a stomach ache? (4)
30. Why did you show _____ so late to the meeting? (2)

Audio Scripts

UNIT 1

CD1 7

I = Interviewer   S = Sally Pearson

I Now, you've probably heard that the Polish community in Britain is growing faster than any other at the moment, but did you know that the total number of Poles living in Britain is now estimated to be three quarters of a million? Well, I'm sure Sally Pearson knows that because she's the Community Development Officer for this region, and she's here in the studio. Welcome Sally.

S Thank you for inviting me.

I Now, that's a huge number of people. Are they all concentrated in a few particular areas?

S No, that's something that's very different about this most recent wave of immigration, it's spread very widely over the whole country. For example, there are 4,000 Poles living in the Highlands of Scotland, working in the fishing and tourist industry.

I That's amazing! So, are these all Poles who've arrived in the UK recently?

S No, they aren't. Many of them have been living here for a long time. About 200,000 Poles settled in Britain after 1945, and about 150,000 of those were still living here in the early 1990s.

I But that's still a huge increase recently then.

S Yes, since the European Union was expanded in 2004, Polish people have taken advantage of the opportunity to relocate here without restrictions.

I Relocating is pretty straightforward then?

S Yes, it is. All they need is a passport, and they can come here to look for a job. In fact, many of them don't have to because a lot of British companies now go out to Poland to recruit people.

I And why are they so keen to do that?

S Well, it's partly economic—what seems like a low wage to British workers can be 2 or 3 times what a Polish worker would take home for a similar job in their own country. However, this is changing as the Polish economy improves.

I But there are other factors as well?

S Yes. As you probably know, Poles have a terrific reputation for being hard workers, and on the whole British employers have found them to be excellent employees.

I But they don't find it so easy to find work in Poland?

S No, they don't. There's a lot of unemployment there, and as I said before, the wages they are offered don't go far, and it's not easy to raise a family on them.

I And what about the downsides? Aren't there always problems when any ethnic minority grows so quickly?

S Yes, there are some, but it helps that Britain is already a very multi-cultural society, and the Polish way of life isn't so very different from our own. Actually, most new Polish arrivals tell me that they get on fine with British people, and that it's people from the older Polish community that seem least friendly towards them.

I Really? Why's that?

S I think it's not unusual actually. People who've struggled hard for many years to settle down in a foreign country are often a bit jealous of newcomers who seem to have it easier than they did. And the older community don't find it easy to identify with the new, younger generation of Poles, and they worry about what their arrival will do for the reputation of Poles living in Britain.

I Well, that doesn't seem to have been a problem, does it?

S No, it doesn't, and I'm sure they all welcome the huge increase in the number of Polish food shops and restaurants in Britain! We know that no matter how happy foreign workers are in Britain, they always miss their own food.

I Yes, and it gives us natives a chance to try yet another kind of foreign food. Anyway, thanks a lot for coming in Sally, and good luck with your development work.

S Thank you.

UNIT 2

CD1 12

L = Linda Davis, presenter
M = Matt Greenberg

L Hello again, and welcome to *What's Cooking?* I'm Linda Davis, and today in the studio we have one of America's best-known and most successful chefs, Matt Greenberg.

M Hi there.

L Matt, you work in one of New York's top hotel kitchens, don't you?

M Yeah, I'm in charge of a great team of chefs there, and I run the kitchen most nights.

L So, what kind of head chef are you then— the typical bad-tempered bully we see on TV, always shouting?

M Mmmm, could be…. Nah, I hardly ever have tantrums, honest! I think running a kitchen does get very stressful if you're passionate about cooking and want to produce the very best, but it actually gives you a real buzz, and I really enjoy the excitement.

L I know what you mean. Now, your background's interesting—you come from England originally, don't you?

M That's right.

L But you're now known for promoting traditional British cooking, which isn't very popular. Why is that?

M Well, I get very frustrated when people say that British cooking isn't very exciting. You know, I tell someone how much I love a good steak pie or a traditional fruit pudding, and they say, "Yeah, fine, but it's all a bit ordinary, isn't it?" Well, I don't agree. I think simple traditional cooking using the best ingredients is never boring and always tasty.

L So, what are you making for us today?

M I'm making a really classic recipe—bread and butter pudding.

L Oh, great—I love bread pudding!

M Yeah, always popular, and it costs next to nothing to make as well. Now, I normally just use raisins in this, but today I'm putting some fresh orange in as well.

L Really? That sounds good. So, you're buttering the bread now—what kind of bread is that?

M It's just an ordinary white loaf, sliced quite thin, with a good sharp bread knife. Right, now I'm heating the milk, cream, and vanilla in a pan, and while that's warming up, I'm whisking the egg yolks and sugar in a bowl.

L How much vanilla extract do you put in?

M I'd say about 5 or 6 drops. And now for the orange—mmm, look at that, a nice organic beauty. These are grown in the Mediterranean, and you can just see all the sunshine that goes into them.

L It does look good, doesn't it? And you're going to peel and chop that?

M No, look, I'm just grating the rind into the raisins.

L OK, and now you're putting the bread into the baking dish.

M That's right, in three layers, with the raisins and orange in between. Now, let's see if that milk's cool enough now—yep, that seems about right—so I'm mixing this into the egg yolks … and now I'm pouring it over the bread. And that's it. Leave it to stand for a while.

L How long?

M About 20–30 minutes, and then put it in the oven for about 30–40 minutes, and that's 350˚F. It needs to be cooked until the top is brown and crispy. Like this one I made earlier.

L Mmm, just the way I like it. Can this be served now?

M You bet!

L Mmmm, that's so good. And people say they don't think much of British cooking…

M Well, they don't know what they're missing, do they?

UNIT 3

CD1 16

C = Carol   R = Richard   A = Anne

C Did you see that TV show about memory last night?

R I can't remember.

C Ha ha.

A No, we didn't. We didn't watch TV last night.

C It was really interesting. There was a part about people's earliest memories that I found absolutely fascinating.

R Why's that?

C They were saying that most people have at least one very vivid memory from around the time when they were three or three and a half, and quite a few people say they can remember things that happened to them when they were one or two years old.

R I find that hard to believe. Can either of you remember anything that early?

C Yes, I can definitely remember something that happened to me when I was about four. My mom says my dad used to carry me a lot on his shoulders at that age, and I absolutely adored it because he was a really big, tall man.

A Yeah, most children love that, don't they?

C Mmm. So, I think I remember being up there, feeling incredibly high up, much higher than anyone else, and maybe it's one of those memories that you do invent later, but I can imagine it now, feeling literally on top of the world.

But that's not actually the strong memory I'm thinking of. That's of this one day when I was with my mom, dad, and older sister, we were walking through some fields near where we lived, and my dad didn't want to pick me up. I was nagging him to carry me, but he said, "No, you're too big for that now." And I can't remember him ever carrying me after that.

A Oh, that's awful!

C Yeah, it was, because, for me it seemed like the end of childhood, and it was so awful and so sudden.

R And what's your earliest memory then, Anne?

A It's from when I was about two and a half, maybe three years old.

R You're kidding! I just can't believe it's possible to remember anything that early.

A Well, I know this isn't something I've just made up because when I asked my mom, she said it had all really happened like that. It was Christmas Eve, and we had this Christmas tree in the living room, and it was an artificial tree, not a real one, and it was all silvery. And my mom took me in to see it when she'd finished putting the lights and decorations on it, and I remember looking up, standing at the foot of it, and looking up… it seemed… to go on forever… the tallest thing I'd ever seen. And it looked so absolutely fabulous, just magical.

C Oh, I can just imagine it!

A And the thing is, we didn't use this tree for another five years or so, and when we got it out again, and I looked at it, I just couldn't believe that it was the same tree. It was pretty small, only about five feet, but to me as a two-year-old it had seemed at least as high as a house!

C That's nice. That really does show what a completely different world small children live in.

R Yeah, that's a good one. I like that. Maybe I'm just jealous because I don't remember anything about my childhood.

A Well, you probably don't want to remember a time when you definitely didn't know everything!

R Come on, Anne, you know, I've always known everything.

UNIT 4

CD1 17

P = Presenter   T = Tony
S = Sarah   A = Andy

P …and it's just coming up to ten minutes past nine and time for our call-in. Today we're asking you which rules you think were made to be broken. And we have Tony, from Brooklyn, on the line. Tony, go ahead.

T I've always hated rules about table manners—drives you crazy. I'll give you an example—you shouldn't put your elbows on the table—why not? Means you can eat more easily, doesn't do any harm, what's the deal?

P You have a point.

T And when you're a kid, you have to eat up everything on your plate. What's that about? If you're full, why should you eat any more? We're actually teaching children to eat too much!

P So, where do you think all this comes from, Tony?

T Dunno. I think people just pick up these rules from their parents—the parents think it's right because they had to do it when they were kids, and then they bring up their own kids the same way. Mindless, stupid rules if you ask me, really gets on my nerves.

P OK, thanks Tony. Sarah, from Manhattan. What rules do you think should be ignored?

S School rules.

P Well, that's a big area. Could you give me an example?

S Yeah, can't leave school during the day.

P What's wrong with that?

S Well, it's just so random. Why aren't I allowed to leave the school to have lunch? Why do we have to stay there all day, like you're in prison or something?

P Come on, Sarah, they can't let you leave whenever you want.

S Well, maybe younger students shouldn't be allowed, but I don't see why older students can't.

P And why is that so important to you?

S Because you have to have some way of showing responsibility, that's something you should encourage, and … [line goes dead]

P Sarah? Can you hear me? Oh, I'm sorry, it looks like Sarah's been cut off. Well, I think she's going to have to stay in school all day anyway. OK, keep the calls coming in, and do try calling again if you don't get through the first time. Andy, from Queens.

A … when you're driving.

P I'm sorry, we seem to be having a few technical problems today. Would you mind repeating that for me, Andy?

A I said I just read the new official advice on what you can and can't do when you're driving.

P Oh, yes, it's not just cell phones that aren't allowed now, is it? They're saying you shouldn't eat at the wheel, aren't they?

A Yeah, and apparently you shouldn't read a map or talk to a passenger while you're driving. It even says you shouldn't listen to loud music in the car! Now, I know it's only using a cell phone that's actually illegal, but if you do these other things, it means that the police could charge you for driving without care and attention.

P Well, to be honest Andy, I think the rules on this should be pretty strict. You have to make sure people are concentrating only on the road when they're driving.

A Yeah, but where do you stop? I mean, you can't stop people talking to each other at all in a car, can you? That's ridiculous!

P No, not really—though at least it would stop some of the fights I have with my wife when I'm driving.

A But what about people changing CDs when they're driving? Surely that's more dangerous than talking to someone, and they don't even mention that.

P Yes, well I know these are only new guidelines, but I think there's going to be a lot of debate on this over the next few months. Anyway, thanks for your call, Andy. Let's take a break and hear about today's weather…

UNIT 5

CD1 19

D = Debbie   J = Jake   S = Steve

D Hi, Jake!

J Debbie! I thought you were back at school already!

D No, not until next week. And I might go back a bit later anyway.

J Come in.

D Is Steve in as well?

J Yes, he just got up. He's meeting his counselor this afternoon to talk about changing majors.

D Not again! Ah, here he is.

S Hi, Debbie! What are you up to?

D Actually, I was wondering if you two were interested in going to the protest at the airport later this week.

J Mmm, I'd be interested in that.

S I didn't know there was one.

D Well, there isn't yet, but they're setting one up tomorrow.

S So, this is all about the third runway they're planning to build then?

D Ah, at least you've heard about that.

S Well, to be honest, I'm not so sure a protest will make any difference on this one.

D What do you mean?

S Well, I'm pretty sure no one's going to cancel their vacation just because a few people have decided to have their own camping vacation at the airport.

D Steve! I'm never sure whether you just don't get it or you enjoy playing the cynic. It's about generating awareness—it's no good having all this talk about stopping global warming and then saying, "Oh, why don't we expand a few airports?"

J Yeah, come on, Steve. I think there's every chance this protest could make a difference. I've been struck by how people's attitudes have changed after all this strange weather we keep having. I think people are beginning to realize they can't take anything for granted with the climate anymore.

S But you know the figures people keep quoting—air travel only accounts for 5% of carbon dioxide emissions.

J And that it's the fastest growing cause of global warming. It's doubled in the last fifteen years.

S So, what's your prediction then—you think they're going to ban air travel someday soon, do you?

J It's not about banning it. It's just saying that it can't continue growing at this rate.

S Fair enough, I suppose. As long as I'm still allowed one trip a year.

D So, what about coming then?

S Is this protest all legal? I'm not going to get involved in anything illegal or violent.

D I don't know if it's legal or illegal, but I'm sure it will be completely non-violent. They're going to build a proper little eco-village—they're even going to bring wind turbines to power it.

J That's pretty cool. As you always say, every little bit helps.

D Let's do it then. We could drive over there on Tuesday.

S I'm afraid Tuesday's no good for me. What about Wednesday?

J Sounds good to me.

D OK, Wednesday it is. I'll pick you both up at 10:00.

UNIT 6

CD1 23

L = Laura   D = Dan

L Hey, I hear you have a new house now. What's it like?

D It's great. It feels so good to have more space after living in that tiny apartment.

L Tell me all about it, how big is the new house then?

D Oh, it's not enormous or anything, but it's just great to have more rooms, especially when the kids are being noisy. But I must admit, the thing I love most about it is my attic room.

L An attic! That sounds wonderfully old-fashioned! I'd love to have an attic in my house.

D Yes. It's a pretty small space actually, but it's so cozy. It has beautiful, old wooden floorboards, and the walls are a rich dark red color, which makes it feel really warm. I just put some very simple furniture in it—a small coffee table and a little two-seater sofa, not much else really …oh, and a lamp. I love to go up there when I want to read, or even to just sit quietly on my own for a while. It's my own space. Nobody else is allowed in.

L Is it light and airy? What kind of windows does it have?

D Well, there's just one small one in the roof—it has a great view of the park, but only if you stand on the coffee table! But that doesn't matter to me because what I like about being in there is that you feel completely cut off from the world. You haven't lived in your house that long, have you? Do you have a favorite room in it?

L Oh yes, I do—it's my bedroom. I like all the rooms in my house, but my bedroom I just love. It's pretty big, and it has a nice soft wool carpet in it, so it's nice to walk around barefoot. I spent ages trying different color paints on the walls, I must have tried a dozen different colors until I finally found exactly the one I wanted. I think getting just the right color for a room is really important, don't you?

D What color is it?

L Blue. A kind of pale blue but a very warm shade—I know that sounds a bit strange, and blues can be quite cold if you don't choose carefully. I really got into color charts and matching colors when I was doing the room. I even made my own cover for the bed—a patchwork-type thing, using squares of material in all different matching shades of blue. It brings everything together beautifully.

D Amazing! I didn't know you had such a creative side to you.

L Well, if you can't find anything you like in the stores, you have to get creative, don't you? And the colors do all look gorgeous, even if I say so myself. I also love it because it's such a bright room, even in winter, especially in the morning when the sun shines straight into it. And the window is one of those huge old-fashioned bay windows you can sit in. I had some cushions made for the window seat, which I just love to sit in, and the first thing I do when I get out of bed is sit on there for a while, just staring out into the world. I like to wake up slowly as I watch the first people setting off for work.

D That sounds nice. That's what I meant about being in my attic—it's a space where I can stare into space and daydream for a while. I think we need to do that at some point in the day.

L Yeah. I do sometimes go up there at other times during the day too. There's hardly any furniture in there apart from the wardrobe, just a chair by the bed. The bed's absolutely huge and it's incredibly comfortable to lie on, so I like to take the newspaper and a mug of hot chocolate up there when I get home from work—to escape!

D I'd be worried about falling asleep!

L Well, I do have a 20-minute nap sometimes. It's the same as with you, I need a place where I can go and have some me-time, before I go downstairs and join the chaos that is my wonderful family.

UNIT 7

CD1 27

C = Counselor   S = Student

C Come in, Jenny. Take a seat.

S Thank you.

C So, you want to find out more about our film courses? Any course in particular?

S Yes. I was thinking of applying for the Degree in Film-Making.

C That's great. Have you read all the admissions requirements? Any questions about those?

S Yes, that's what I wanted to ask about first— what kind of experience do you need to do that program?

C Well, first of all I'll say that all our students are people who've shown they have a real passion for film.

S That's certainly true for me. I've always been crazy about anything to do with film.

C Great. Most of those who start the degree have been making their own films for some time and have worked a lot with other people in the process—teamwork is such an important part of film-making.

S Well, I have made a couple of short films. That was on the program I was doing.

C What program was that? Where did you do it?

S I just finished a part-time Film Studies program at my local college.

C Good for you! Did you find it helpful?

S Yes, it was really informative—is it useful to have a qualification like that?

C Well, it certainly doesn't do any harm, but this is actually a very practical program, not a very academic one! It has to be said, no one's ever been employed in the film industry just because they've completed a course—it's all about practical experience.

S And do your graduates generally manage to get jobs in film?

C Oh yes, they've been employed in all areas of the industry—feature films, TV drama, commercials, pop videos, you name it, they've done it. We have a couple of recent graduates who just released their own low budget feature film, and it's already won an award. In all, about 70% of our recent graduates are working in the business at the moment.

S That's amazing!

C So have you had any experience of directing—camera planning, scheduling, finding and working with actors?

S No, the films I made were real life documentaries, so there wasn't much need for that kind of direction.

C That's a shame. Did you use music on them? The degree has a class on the use of music in film, and you get experience working with a composer.

S Actually, I only had title music on my films—I've never gone into music much.

C OK. Not to worry. Do you have any idea which area of film you'd like to specialize in once you've graduated?

S No, I haven't decided yet. I think I need to know more about all the different areas.

C Fair enough. You know, I'm beginning to think it might be a good idea for you to do our Foundation program first, before you think about applying for the degree. That would give you a very good basis for the degree later on.

S What do you do in the Foundation program?

C You learn all the basics—scriptwriting, lighting, camera work, and direction. It'll give you enough experience in each area to decide which one you want to specialize in.

S That sounds like a good idea. How long is the program?

C You can do it in a month, during the summer. We're just about to start interviews for that, in May and June—ask for an appointment in reception. I think you'll enjoy it—you should have a lot in common with the other students on that program. We work hard here, but we do make sure we have fun, too!

S Great. I'll go and put my name down for that now. Thanks a lot for your time.

C You're welcome. See you in the summer, I hope. Bye.

S Thanks. I hope so too. Bye.

UNIT 8

CD1 31

I = Interviewer C = Carla Simpson

I In this next part of Film Focus, we are going to look at a less well-known aspect of the movie industry—now, we're all familiar with the term "stuntman," but we don't often hear about "stunt*women*." They do exist, of course, and my final guest today is Carla Simpson, who's succeeded in becoming one of Hollywood's top stuntwomen. Hello and welcome, Carla Simpson.

C Thanks.

I So, Carla, tell me, why is it so easy to forget that stuntwomen exist?

C Well, you need to remember that until relatively recently you didn't often see women doing dangerous things in action movies; it was very much a man's world, and if a woman *was* involved, the stunt would still be done by a man.

I What? Dressed up?

C Yes. Well, it's not that difficult to make a man look like a woman, is it? As long as the camera doesn't get too close! But of course these days we expect women to do the stunts, just like the guys, and stuntwomen are actually very much in demand right now. Ever since movies like *Lara Croft Tomb Raider* and the *Matrix* films, there have been lots more high-powered action roles for women, which is great!

I And had you always planned to become a stuntwoman?

C No, I'd never planned to at all—I wanted to be an actor originally. I managed to get into acting school, but I really wasn't very good at it. My teacher knew I was a bit of an adrenaline junkie, and she told me to think about doing stunt work. It just grew from there.

I Were you a bit of a tomboy as a child?

C Oh yes, I was pretty fearless, and I remember climbing trees and jumping off high walls when I was very young. I was always trying to beat the boys, and I've always loved doing extreme sports. That's the great thing—I get paid for doing it now! It's unbelievable!

I So, how do you actually go about becoming a stuntwoman? Are there schools you can go to?

C Not really, it's more a case of finding a trainer to work with. You *do* have to be very highly trained, in an incredible range of skills—driving, and that includes motorcycles, climbing, falling from high buildings, using weapons, then there's fire work, hand fighting, horse work—especially falling off, of course.

I And you have to be able to do *all* those?

C Uh, you don't *have* to, but the more the better. That way you get more work. But most stunt people tend to specialize in one or two areas. For example, I don't mind doing fire work, but I'd rather not do it, whereas I actually enjoy doing high falls.

I But do you ever get scared when you're doing some stunts?

C Well, you know, there's nothing wrong with being afraid of getting hurt badly, and many stunts are life-threatening if they're not fully prepared. That's the key to it, serious preparation. If things aren't properly prepared, I complain, and you need to make sure that everyone is concentrating 100% during a stunt. You minimize the risks.

I Have you been hurt?

C You often get hurt, even on simple stunts, which is why they can't let the actors do them—it's too expensive for them to be off work, even for a day or two. But in the stunt world, we only call it being hurt if you need an ambulance.

I Mmm, it doesn't sound like my idea of fun, I must say.

C Maybe not, but you know, when people ask me about being scared, I always tell them, what really scares me is the idea of wasting your life, not living it to the fullest—that's a truly terrifying thought to me.

I That's a great note to end on. Thanks a lot, Carla.

C Thank you.

UNIT 9

CD1 35

E = Elaine P = Peter

E I bumped into Suzie in town today, and she was telling me that ...

P Hold on, I'll get that. Hello?
Oh, wonderful, I'm thrilled.
Good-bye.

E Who on earth was that?

P Oh, one of those stupid automated messages. "You have won a prize. Call this number to claim it."

E Oh no. I can't believe anyone would really fall for that. Apparently, if you call back, the prizes are worthless, but they charge you as much as $50 for the call.

P Yeah, I know. But there must be plenty of people stupid enough to believe it, otherwise they wouldn't do it, would they?

E I guess not. You know I read somewhere recently that in the U.S. more than five million people lost money to conmen last year.

P That's amazing! There's a guy in my office who got phished last week, and he fell for it.

E Phishing's when they send you fake e-mails, right?

P Yeah, this was one that looked like it was from his bank, saying they needed to update the security details on his account. There was a link that sent him to a website that looked just like his bank's, and of course, he had to enter his old security details before entering new ones.

E Mmm. I must admit, I might have fallen for that one. It's clever, because they're using your insecurity about being conned to con you!

P Yeah. And they can empty your bank account long before you know anything about it.

E Well, someone at my work had his credit card stolen from his jacket, hanging on the back of the office door. He hadn't even noticed, so he was really happy when the bank called him and said that they'd just stopped the criminal trying to use it. Of course, they also wanted to check some security details to make sure it was his card.

P Uh oh! I've guessed what's coming next!

E Yup—he told them his PIN number, and of course, it was actually the thief calling, and he went right away on a very long shopping trip.

P Oh, that's mean. It's obvious a bank would never have asked for his PIN number, but you wouldn't register that at the time, would you? You'd be in a bit of panic after being told that your wallet's been stolen.

E Absolutely. It's useful to hear about these scams, though, isn't it? I mean, if they tried that one on *me* now, at least I'd know about it.

P Yeah. Well, the best one I've ever seen was on that TV show where they film actors doing scams on the public. This actor, a big guy, walks into a museum wearing a black suit and a white shirt and stops in a corridor in the middle of the museum. Out of his pocket he pulls a security guard's cap and an official-looking badge, which he hangs around his neck. And he starts stopping people and says he has to check them, searching their pockets for anything dangerous.

E And somehow I suspect there was less in their pockets at the end of the search?

P That's right. He got three wallets full of cash and credit cards in about five minutes. And it was a long time before any of them noticed, because they were walking around the rest of the museum.

E You see, I would have believed him, definitely. It's the authority thing with people in a uniform, you just obey them automatically.

P Yeah, and even if somewhere inside you did feel a little suspicious, you wouldn't want to make a scene in public, would you?

E Certainly not! But honestly, if we're not careful, we'll end up being suspicious of everyone. Still, I suppose it's good to be on your guard.

UNIT 10

CD1 38

M = Mark   **A = Amy**

M Hi, Amy! How's it going?

A Hi, Mark. Oh, OK. I'm just a little annoyed with myself because I left my umbrella on the bus. It was a really good one too.

M Someone might hand it in, you never know.

A Oh, I doubt it. And anyway, it's such an effort to go to the Lost and Found office—and I don't even know where it is—and there's probably loads of paperwork involved in getting it back.

M Well, you're in luck. I have a friend who works in the bus station, and I think he has to deal with lost property sometimes. I can give him a call, and if it's been handed in, he could have it ready for you to pick up.

A Aw, that would be great, thanks.

M So, which umbrella should I tell him to look out for—the pink girlie one I assume?

A Yes, of course—it's a Barbie umbrella. Actually, it's a very classy-looking black and white umbrella with a silver point. It's pretty big—it looks like a golfing umbrella. And … it has a white handle with a black stripe down the side of it.

M Excuse me! I'll wait a couple of hours and then call him.

A I bet they get tons of umbrellas left on buses, don't they?

M Yeah. I think it might be the most common thing, I can't remember. I read something on the Internet a couple of weeks ago about the things that people most often leave on public transportation. Let me see if I can find it again … Yes, here it is. Ah, umbrellas are number three on the list. What do you think is the most common?

A Bags?

M Oooh, close. That's number two—especially shopping bags. Yeah, I've done that—put it on the floor under your feet, and you've forgotten all about it by the time you get off.

A Is it sunglasses?

M Well, it doesn't say *sun*glasses, but glasses in general are fourth on the list.

A I can't think what it is then.

M Coats and jackets.

A Oh, that does surprise me. They seem too big to forget about, and you wouldn't put them on the floor. What about cell phones? Are they on the list?

M Yup, they're number five. [laughs] It says that they leave them switched on so that people can call them, but everyone who calls in thinks that the person who's answering is a thief, so they get a lot of abuse at first! Now, what about laptops?

A Surely people don't leave those on buses and trains very often, do they?

M Well, they're not on this list. But the article says there is a place where laptops are often lost. See if you can guess where it is.

A Taxis?

M No—it's airports.

A What? In the departure lounge?

M No. It sounds unbelievable, but it's people forgetting to pick their laptops up again after they've put them through the X-ray machine.

A No! And I thought I was stupid. I'd never forgive myself if I did that.

M Oh, come on, it is a pretty stressful time, sorting out your coat, cell phone, belt, shoes, money—and all those security guards staring at you. People can't get out of there quick enough.

A But they must realize they've left them behind before long. Why don't they just go back and ask?

M Maybe they don't have time to go all the way back to the X-ray machines by the time they've realized. And it says that like you, most people don't even contact the Lost and Found about it—they just assume someone will have stolen it.

A It's terrible how little we trust each other these days, isn't it? Anyway, we'll see. If someone hands my umbrella in, I'll promise to have more faith in human nature.

UNIT 11

Dear Ruth,

I am fourteen years old, and I have a big problem with my younger brother, Cal, who's 8. We fight all the time. It's terrible, I know, but I think I hate him. He follows me everywhere, and he wants to use all my things, especially my computer. He ruins everything I'm doing. If I'm with my friends, he always wants to be with us, and when I tell him to go away he goes crying to our mother. My parents always take his side. He's so spoiled he gets everything he wants. My mom says she can't understand why I don't want him with me and my friends, but we can't talk freely with him hanging around all the time. My dad says I should play with him more and let him use my computer, but he just plays his silly games on it and screams if I want to use it for my school work. He doesn't have many friends. Nobody at his school likes him, and I know why—he cries if he doesn't win every game, and he fights with the other children. My parents think he can do no wrong. What can I do?
Yours,
Luke Basset

Dear Ruth,

My husband and I and our two sons are a happy and loving family. Ten months ago, after years of saving our money, we moved to the house of our dreams. However, our lives are now being made miserable by the behavior of our neighbors, Mr. and Mrs. Fletcher. They play loud music until late at night. It's so loud that our children can't sleep. When we asked them to turn it down they refused. They don't have any children, and they say that ours make too much noise when they're playing in the backyard. Also, they have refused to cut the hedge on their side of the fence. It is now huge and stops all the sunlight getting into our backyard. One of the reasons we bought the house was because of the beautiful backyard, and now we can't use it. We've tried to talk to them about this too, but they say that they can do what they want in their backyard. We don't want to move, but we're going crazy. What can we do?
Yours,
Jane Iverson

CD1 41

J = Jake   **D = Dad**

J Dad, can you help me with my English homework?

D Sure, what's it on?

J We're doing *Romeo and Juliet*.

D Ah, that's funny. I was listening to a radio program on Shakespeare in the car today. About how he might not have actually written the plays.

J You're kidding!

D No. Do they ever talk about that at school?

J No.

D Well, I think there've always been theories that Shakespeare couldn't have written them—and to be honest—I did find this program pretty convincing, even though I haven't read any of his plays since I was in school.

J But look, it says here in black and white, *Romeo and Juliet* by William Shakespeare. Must be true.

D Not really. Don't believe everything you read. They said on this program that no one can come up with any hard evidence that Shakespeare was a writer—there are documents referring to him but only as an actor and a businessman. And apparently he didn't write his name like that—he spelled it in different ways, but in all his signatures it's "Shaksper"—S-H-A-K-S-P-E-R.

J That's funny actually, because I can never remember if there's an "e" at the end of his name or not. He could just have been even worse at spelling than I am.

D No, that's not possible, Jake. But some people argue that Shakespeare couldn't have had the education you'd need to write all those plays. There's so much world knowledge in them—well, you must know that from having to work out all the references, you know, to history, law, music, Italian culture, all the foreign languages in them. But Shakespeare was from a pretty ordinary background, you know, so at best he must have gone to the local grammar school and left at sixteen. He never went to college.

J Really? But weren't universities just for aristocrats in those days anyway? And didn't they study weird subjects too?—Latin grammar and astronomy—ugh!

D Yeah, well, of course, you're right—very few people did go in those days and yes, ordinary people weren't allowed to go.

J But couldn't he have found out all that information for himself some other way?

D What, on the Internet?

J Yeah, ha ha, alright, it wouldn't have been so easy.

D And the other thing is, there's nothing in the plays about Shakespeare's own background, you know, Stratford, stuff from his own life.

J Well, writers do make things up when they're writing, Dad.

D Yeah, but there's always *something* that comes from their own life. With Shakespeare, nothing we can see. And—this I did find amazing—apparently Shakespeare's own daughters couldn't read or write! Not what you'd expect from a literary genius, is it?

J So who do these people think must have written these plays then?

D Um, what was his name? Edward somebody ... De Vere, I think, the Earl of Oxford.

J Is there any proof?

D Not really, but they said there's a lot in the plays that's similar to events in *his* life, and being an aristocrat, he would have had the right background, university, lots of foreign travel.

J And was he definitely a writer then?

D Well, apparently there are lots of documents referring to him as a writer of great poems and plays, but there isn't a single play published in his name. That's the big flaw in the argument.

J Right. Well, at least I can forget this homework now.

D What do you mean?

J Well, they can't expect me to write an essay on Shakespeare's style if they can't even prove he wrote this play, can they?

D Mmm. I don't think they'll buy that argument at school—remember it's only a theory, and there's no proof that Shakespeare *didn't* write the plays. Sorry, Jake, come on, let's have a look at what you have to write.

UNIT 12

J= Julia   C = Colin

J Oh, you're back. You've been gone forever. What were you up to?

C The supermarket was absolutely packed. I'd forgotten Friday night is always so crowded.

J Well, rather you than me. Did you get the brown rice?

C No, I got white rice. You didn't say you wanted brown.

J Yes, I did. I distinctly remember saying it to you as you went out. Anyway, that's what this recipe says we have to use.

C I never heard you say anything about brown rice.

J But I did. I told you that we'd run out of brown rice and I needed it for this ... Oh, never mind! You obviously weren't listening to me—again.

C Yes, I was, honestly. I just don't remember you saying anything about brown rice.

J You just don't listen to me. Don't deny it.

C Well, that's not true—or at least only when you're nagging.

J I presume that means whenever I complain about anything. Then I'm nagging and being unreasonable.

C Well, sometimes you *can* be a little unreasonable when we argue.

J Oh, so it's unreasonable to criticize you, is it? I am so sure I asked you to get brown rice, but you're never going to admit you weren't listening—as usual! Oh look—we just seem to be going around in circles again! Let's forget it.

C Alright, I'm sorry, we all make mistakes, and we're both tired and hungry after a long day at work. Let's just eat and then watch TV. Did you record my program?

J Sorry, what program? You didn't say you wanted me to record anything.

C But it's Thursday. I always record the game on Thursday, you said you'd record it for me whenever I'm not here.

J Well, come on, you didn't remind me to. Honestly, I can't remember everything, you know.

C True!

J Look, I'm sorry—let's call it quits! I hate it when we argue like this.

C Me too. Anyway, I can live without football for a week I suppose. Maybe I'll go on the Internet and book that weekend in Boston we were talking about.

J Ah, I meant to say earlier—I've changed my mind about that.

C What do you mean?

J Well, you see, I was talking to Jane today and she told me that she and Fred had had a really awful time in Boston last weekend. She said the weather was absolutely terrible—freezing cold and wet.

C Does it really matter what your sister and her boring husband think? Lots of people have told me that Boston's a wonderful place. It has so much, the buildings, the atmosphere …

J I know, I know. It's just that I'd rather wait until it's a bit warmer. We could go in the summer—maybe for the Fourth of July. Actually, Lisa at work said that she'd been to Washington, DC last weekend, and she thought it was one of the most beautiful cities she'd ever seen. And there's lots to do and see, and it should be a little warmer than Boston at this time of year.

C OK, I give in! But you better make up your mind soon, you know if we don't book soon, the train tickets will be very expensive. We have to book three weeks before we want to go to get the best price.

J OK, where do *you* want to go?

C I suppose I don't really mind. Let's go to Washington, DC then. It is supposed to be really nice. I think it said in the newspaper that there was a festival there next month that might be worth going to. I'll check that out, and maybe we can decide when we'd like to go.

J Great. Thanks, darling. Oh, Colin, would you like a brown rice salad made with white rice?

C Sounds wonderful. All that arguing has made me hungry!

Verb Patterns

Verbs + *-ing*	
adore can't stand don't mind enjoy finish imagine loathe	doing swimming cooking

Note

We often use the verb *go + -ing* for sports and activities.
> I **go swimming** *every day.*
> I **go shopping** *on weekends.*

Verbs + preposition + *-ing*	
give up look forward to succeed in think of	doing

Verbs + *to* + infinitive	
afford agree choose dare decide expect forget help hope learn manage mean need offer plan promise refuse seem want would hate would like would love would prefer	to do to come to cook

Notes

1. *Help* and *dare* can be used without *to*.
   > We **helped clean up** *the kitchen.*
   > *They didn't* **dare disagree** *with him.*

2. *Have to* for obligation.
   > I **have to wear** *a uniform.*

3. *Used to* for past habits.
   > I **used to eat greasy food**, *but I stopped last year.*

Verbs + sb + *to* + infinitive		
advise allow ask beg encourage expect force help invite need order persuade remind tell want warn would like	me him them someone	to do to go to come

Note

Help can be used without *to*.
> I **helped** *him* **do** *the dishes.*

Verbs + sb + infinitive (no *to*)		
help let make	her us	do

Notes

1. *To* is used with *make* in the passive.
   > *We were* **made to work** *hard.*

2. *Let* cannot be used in the passive. *Allowed to* is used instead.
   > *She was* **allowed to leave.**

Verbs + *-ing* or *to* + infinitive (with little or no change in meaning)	
begin continue hate like love prefer start	doing to do

Verbs + *-ing* or *to* + infinitive (with a change in meaning)	
remember stop try	doing to do

Notes

1. *I **remember mailing** the letter.*
   (= I have a memory now of a past action: mailing the letter.)

   *I **remembered to mail** the letter.*
   (= I reminded myself to mail the letter. I didn't forget.)

2. *I **stopped drinking** coffee.*
   (= I gave up the habit.)

   *I **stopped to drink** a coffee.*
   (= I stopped doing something else in order to have a cup of coffee.)

3. *I **tried to sleep**.*
   (= I wanted to sleep, but it was difficult.)

   *I **tried counting** sheep and **drinking** a glass of warm milk.*
   (= These were possible ways of getting to sleep.)

Irregular verbs

Base form	Past Simple	Past participle	Base form	Past Simple	Past participle
be	was/were	been	eave	left	left
beat	beat	beaten	lend	lent	lent
become	became	become	let	let	let
begin	began	begun	lie	lay	lain
bend	bent	bent	light	lighted/lit	lighted/lit
bite	bit	bitten	lose	lost	lost
blow	blew	blown	make	made	made
break	broke	broken	mean	meant	meant
bring	brought	brought	meet	met	met
build	built	built	must	had to	had to
buy	bought	bought	pay	paid	paid
can	could	been able	put	put	put
catch	caught	caught	read /rid/	read /red/	read /red/
choose	chose	chosen	ride	rode	ridden
come	came	come	ring	rang	rung
cost	cost	cost	rise	rose	risen
cut	cut	cut	run	ran	run
dig	dug	dug	say	said	said
do	did	done	see	saw	seen
draw	drew	drawn	sell	sold	sold
dream	dreamed	dreamed	send	sent	sent
drink	drank	drunk	set	set	set
drive	drove	driven	shake	shook	shaken
eat	ate	eaten	shine	shone	shone
fall	fell	fallen	shoot	shot	shot
feed	fed	fed	show	showed	shown
feel	felt	felt	shut	shut	shut
fight	fought	fought	sing	sang	sung
find	found	found	sink	sank	sunk
fit	fit	fit	sit	sat	sat
fly	flew	flown	sleep	slept	slept
forget	forgot	forgotten	slide	slid	slid
forgive	forgave	forgiven	speak	spoke	spoken
freeze	froze	frozen	spend	spent	spent
get	got	got	spoil	spoiled	spoiled
give	gave	given	spread	spread	spread
go	went	been/gone	stand	stood	stood
grow	grew	grown	steal	stole	stolen
hang	hanged/hung	hanged/hung	stick	stuck	stuck
have	had	had	swim	swam	swum
hear	heard	heard	take	took	taken
hide	hid	hidden	teach	taught	taught
hit	hit	hit	tear	tore	torn
hold	held	held	tell	told	told
hurt	hurt	hurt	think	thought	thought
keep	kept	kept	throw	threw	thrown
kneel	knelt	knelt	understand	understood	understood
know	knew	known	wake	woke	woken
lay	laid	laid	wear	wore	worn
lead	led	led	win	won	won
learn	learned	learned	write	wrote	written

Phonetic symbols

Consonants			
1	/p/	as in	**pen** /pɛn/
2	/b/	as in	**big** /bɪg/
3	/t/	as in	**tea** /ti/
4	/d/	as in	**do** /du/
5	/k/	as in	**cat** /kæt/
6	/g/	as in	**go** /goʊ/
7	/f/	as in	**five** /faɪv/
8	/v/	as in	**very** /ˈvɛri/
9	/s/	as in	**son** /sʌn/
10	/z/	as in	**zoo** /zu/
11	/l/	as in	**live** /lɪv/
12	/m/	as in	**my** /maɪ/
13	/n/	as in	**nine** /naɪn/
14	/h/	as in	**happy** /ˈhæpi/
15	/r/	as in	**red** /rɛd/
16	/y/	as in	**yes** /yɛs/
17	/w/	as in	**want** /wɒnt/
18	/θ/	as in	**thanks** /θæŋks/
19	/ð/	as in	**the** /ðə/
20	/ʃ/	as in	**she** /ʃi/
21	/ʒ/	as in	**television** /ˈtɛlɪvɪʒn/
22	/tʃ/	as in	**child** /tʃaɪld/
23	/dʒ/	as in	**Japan** /dʒəˈpæn/
24	/ŋ/	as in	**English** /ˈɪŋglɪʃ/

Vowels			
25	/i/	as in	**see** /si/
26	/ɪ/	as in	**his** /hɪz/
27	/ɛ/	as in	**ten** /tɛn/
28	/æ/	as in	**stamp** /stæmp/
29	/ɑ/	as in	**father** /ˈfɑðər/
30	/ɔ/	as in	**saw** /sɔ/
31	/ɒ/	as in	**hot** /hɒt/
32	/ʊ/	as in	**book** /bʊk/
33	/u/	as in	**you** /yu/
34	/ʌ/	as in	**sun** /sʌn/
35	/ə/	as in	**about** /əˈbaʊt/
36	/eɪ/	as in	**name** /neɪm/
37	/aɪ/	as in	**my** /maɪ/
38	/ɔɪ/	as in	**boy** /bɔɪ/
39	/aʊ/	as in	**how** /haʊ/
40	/oʊ/	as in	**go** /goʊ/
41	/ər/	as in	**bird** /bərd/
42	/ɪr/	as in	**near** /nɪr/
43	/ɛr/	as in	**hair** /hɛr/
44	/ar/	as in	**car** /kar/
45	/ɔr/	as in	**more** /mɔr/
46	/ʊr/	as in	**tour** /tʊr/

SPOTLIGHT ON TESTING

Unit 1 | Identifying differences

Details about differences

Some test questions about differences ask for specific details. Exactly how are two things different? Listen for comparatives (e.g., *smaller*, *drier*, *more expensive*). Also listen for contrast signals like *but* or *however*.

1 Listening for details about differences

A. AUDIO FILE 🔊 Listen to the interview. According to Tom, how is Florida different from Montana? Write *T* for true or *F* for false.

1. ____ People do not hike in Florida.

2. ____ Florida is flatter than Montana.

3. ____ People in Montana do not like their neighbors.

4. ____ People in Florida live closer together.

5. ____ Winters in Florida are better than winters in Montana.

B. AUDIO FILE 🔊 Circle the letter of the best answer to each question. Then listen again and check your answers.

1. Tom says hiking in Montana is better than in Florida because ____.
   a. Montana has more trees
   b. in Montana you can see farther
   c. Montana's weather is warmer

2. Tom says houses in Montana are ____ than in Florida.
   a. less expensive
   b. farther apart
   c. closer together

3. Tom thinks that the air in Florida is ____ than the air in Montana.
   a. drier
   b. colder
   c. wetter

Wh- questions about details

Listening and reading tests often use *wh-* question words (*what, where, how,* etc.) to ask about differences. Be especially prepared for questions starting with *how*, *in what way*, and *what is the difference*.

2 *Wh-* questions related to differences

AUDIO FILE 🔊 Listen to the interview again. Check (✓) the best answer.

1. In what way are Florida neighbors different from Montana neighbors?
   a. ☐ They see each other more.   b. ☐ They know each other less.

2. What is one difference between horse riding in Montana and in Florida?
   a. ☐ No one in Florida rides.   b. ☐ Fewer people in Florida ride.

3. How is Florida weather different from Montana weather?
   a. ☐ Montana has drier air.   b. ☐ Montana has warmer summers.

Strategies for taking the: TOEFL® Test   TOEIC® Test   IELTS™ Test

3 Finding answers to *wh-* questions about differences

Read the article. Circle the letter of the best answer.

1. Which gas makes up more of the air we breathe?
   a. nitrogen   b. oxygen

2. Who first became president at an earlier age?
   a. Kennedy   b. Roosevelt

3. How is the inland taipan different from other snakes?
   a. It's deadlier.   b. It's more poisonous.

4. In what way was Genghis Khan different from other leaders?
   a. He had more children.   b. He had children in more places.

5. How are the Himalayas different from the Appalachians?
   a. They are rising up.   b. They are wearing down.

Did You Know?

- The most common gas in the air we breathe (about 78 percent of it) is nitrogen (N). Oxygen (0_2) makes up only about 21 percent of air.

- John F. Kennedy was the youngest person ever elected president of the United States (43 years old). However, Theodore Roosevelt was the youngest president. He was 42 in 1901 when he became president—not by being elected, but by taking over when President William McKinley died. He was actually elected president in 1904, at the age of 45.

- The most poisonous snake in the world is the inland taipan of Australia. One bite has enough poison to kill 100 people. But it is not the deadliest snake. It almost never bites people. In fact, there is no recorded case of a person dying from an inland taipan bite.

- DNA researchers believe at least 16 million people throughout the world are descended from a single 14th-century warrior—the Mongol leader Genghis Khan. He had hundreds of children, but so did other leaders of his time. He was different from other leaders because of how widely his influence spread. He left behind children wherever his armies marched—across much of Asia and into Eastern Europe.

- The highest mountains on Earth, the Himalayas, get higher every year. Older mountain ranges, like the Appalachians of North America, get lower as the weather wears them down. Forces in the earth are still pushing the much younger Himalayas upward by about two inches per year.

4 Check your understanding

Read the article again. Write *T* for true or *F* for false.

1. ____ Theodore Roosevelt was not elected president.

2. ____ As far as we know, an inland taipan has never killed anyone.

3. ____ People related to Genghis Khan live all around the world.

4. ____ The highest mountains on Earth are still getting higher.

> Scan for key words in a *wh-* question to find answers. For example, in "Which gas makes up more of the air we breathe?" *gas*, *more*, and *air* are key words. The answer could be near these words in a reading test.

5 Skills in review

Look at the descriptions of three people on p. 2 of the Workbook. Write 5 *wh-* questions about their differences. Answer your questions.

Usual actions vs. actions right now

Some test questions ask whether an action usually happens or is happening now. Try to recognize present simple and present continuous verbs in a reading or listening passage. Adverbs like *now*, *currently*, *often*, or *every day* can also help.

1 Understanding usual and current actions

Read Bob's journal entries. According to Bob, which actions <u>usually</u> happen? Write *U*. Which actions are happening <u>now</u> (at the time Bob is writing)? Write *N*.

1. ____ Bob / live in Atlanta
2. ____ Sky / fill with bright stars
3. ____ Bob, Al, and Cindy / camp together
4. ____ Al / manage writers
5. ____ Young readers / get news online
6. ____ Bob / look forward to hearing from Al

Bob Jameson's Journal: Walking and Writing

Sunday, September 12

I live in Atlanta, but now I'm exploring a larger world. This is my first day on the Appalachian Trail. I plan to walk as far as possible in two weeks. The trail is beautiful—deep forests and high mountaintops. I am writing this journal entry at about 9:30 at night. The sun is going down. The sky is filling up with bright stars. I am happy. I have a strong tent, good boots, and an open mind.

Monday, September 13

Today I met Al and Cindy, a couple from Chicago. He works for an advertising agency. She's a photographer. We're camping together tonight in a little shelter. As I write this, Al is cooking some spaghetti for tonight's dinner. We talked a little bit today about their work. He manages people who write TV commercials. Sometimes she takes pictures for commercials, but mostly she takes photographs of nature. They are often printed in national magazines.

Tuesday, September 14

Al, Cindy, and I walked together for a few miles this morning. I told them that I write for a newspaper in Atlanta, but my articles are usually published online. They were very interested, so I explained a little bit. Most young readers get their news online. Newspapers are trying to reach these people. Hard-copy news—on real paper—is being replaced by electronic news. We had lunch together at noon, and then Al and Cindy took a different path. They are walking toward the city of Asheville. I am continuing straight north along the trail. Al said he might call me later. He is looking for new writers for his company, especially writers with online experience. That could be cool. I'm looking forward to hearing from him.

Strategies for taking the: **TOEFL® Test**   **TOEIC® Test**   **IELTS™ Test**

Who or what performs an action? Who or what is affected by the action? Test questions about *voice*—active or passive—ask you to understand this.

2 Active and passive verbs in the present

Read the journal again. Check (✓) each correct sentence.

1. ____ Spaghetti is cooking dinner.

2. ____ National magazines print Cindy's pictures.

3. ____ Hard-copy news is replacing electronic news.

Grammar questions on some tests ask you to choose the best verb form. Your choices may include simple, continuous, active, and passive verb forms. Try to learn all these forms of each verb you study.

3 Choosing verb forms

AUDIO FILE 🔊 Listen to the presentation. Circle the letter of the best verb to fill in the blank.

1. The speaker sees that many students ____ their hands.
   a. are held up   b. are holding up   c. is holding up   d. are being held up

2. Common jobs usually ____ on the Human Resources Web site.
   a. list   b. are listed   c. are listing   d. are being listed

3. The Biology department often ____ students for jobs in labs.
   a. hires   b. is hiring   c. is hired   d. is being hired

4. At today's session, the speaker ____ to help students find jobs.
   a. try   b. tries   c. are trying   d. is trying

4 Check your understanding

AUDIO FILE 🔊 Listen to the presentation again. Write *T* for true or *F* for false.

1. ____ Students cannot take jobs that are listed on the Human Resources site.

2. ____ Some students are hired by the college and others are hired by departments.

3. ____ Most student workers are hired by the Biology department.

4. ____ Jobs are easier to find at the start of a semester.

5 Skills in review

Look at the article about the U.S. on p. 13 of the Workbook. How does your country's economy compare? Use similar verbs to describe your country's economy.

> In verb-choice questions, look at the subject. Is it singular or plural? This can eliminate some choices. For example, "The students ____ dinner" cannot be completed with *eats* or *is eating*. Why? Because the subject, *the students*, is plural.

Unit 3 | Details in narratives

Historical narratives are very common in reading and listening tests. Questions about them may focus on dates and places. In your mind or in your notes, try to make these connections: **event + time + place**.

1 Listening for where and when

AUDIO FILE 🔊 Listen to the lecture. Write no more than three words or one number in each blank.

1. The founders of the Amana Colonies came to the United States from _____.

2. Inspirationists bought land in east-central _____.

3. In the year _____ , the Inspirationists moved to their present location.

4. Amana residents ate their meals together in _____.

5. In 1932, the Inspirationists voted to set up a company called _____.

6. In _____ , George Foerstner set up a company called Amana Refrigeration, Inc.

Completing summaries by filling in blanks

A summary test question could be a paragraph with blanks to fill. Scan the original reading for each word from the list of possible answers. It may appear in a context similar to one of the blanks.

2 Summarizing a narrative

AUDIO FILE 🔊 Listen to the lecture again. Fill each blank with a word from the list.

beliefs	moved	private	share	together

In the 1840s, a German religious group called the Inspirationists (1) _____ to the United States. One of their main (2) _____ was that people in a community should (3) _____ everything they own. They set up the Amana Colonies in Iowa. Everyone in the community ate and worked (4) _____. In the 1930s, they ended their joint ownership of property. They became shareholders in a (5) _____ company called the Amana Society.

Completing summaries by choosing sentences

In some tests, you complete a summary by choosing sentences from a list. Choose the sentences that express the main ideas of a reading.

3 Prose Summary

Read the article. The first sentence of a summary is given to you. Choose three more sentences from the list to complete the summary. Check (✔) the sentences you choose.

> **Legends tell of a great king named Arthur who led Britons against the Saxons in England.**

1. ____ Legends tell about Arthur, his knights, and life in Camelot.

2. ____ King Arthur's castle, Camelot, was a model society, with brave knights and fair leadership.

Strategies for taking the: (**TOEFL** Test) (**TOEIC** Test) (**IELTS** Test)

3. ____ The Saxons came from Germany.

4. ____ Most of the Arthur legends were first written down in the 15th century.

5. ____ Arthur and the knights often went on quests to perform great deeds.

6. ____ The end of Camelot's greatness came after Queen Guinevere had a love affair with Sir Lancelot.

The Legendary King Arthur

According to British legends, Arthur, the son of King Uther Pendragon, was hidden away as a boy, so he would be safe from enemies. He was recognized as a king only after he pulled a magical sword out of a stone. Arthur was a Briton. He came from a people who ruled much of England before Saxons invaded from Germany. As king, Arthur gathered great knights to help him fight the Saxons—the famous Knights of the Round Table. Arthur's castle, Camelot, was a model society. The knights were true and noble, the king was powerful but fair, and the people were treated well.

Over time, countless legends built up around Arthur's glorious court. Arthur's beautiful wife, Queen Guinevere, and his most trusted knight, Sir Lancelot, are the lead characters in many of these legends. Besides fighting Saxons, the knights, and sometimes the king himself, went on quests. These were difficult journeys meant to accomplish a noble deed. The most famous was the Quest for the Holy Grail, a magical cup with great religious meaning. Many knights, including Lancelot, tried but failed to find the grail. Sir Galahad eventually found it, his reward for living a pure and holy life. Other quests involved such good deeds as rescuing prisoners, killing monsters, and driving away evil wizards.

The great days of Camelot ended after King Arthur discovered that Queen Guinevere had a love affair with Sir Lancelot. To enforce the law, Arthur was forced to punish his dear friend and his beloved wife. The Knights of the Round Table left Camelot and went their separate ways. Eventually, Arthur went into battle against a former knight of Camelot, Sir Mordred. In some versions of the legend, both Arthur and Mordred are killed. In others, Arthur does not actually die, but is taken to the magical island of Avalon. There he waits for a chance to return and re-establish Camelot.

4 Check your understanding

Read the article again. Write *T* for true or *F* for false, according to the reading.

1. ____ Arthur was not recognized as a king when he was a little boy.

2. ____ Sir Lancelot went on a quest to find the Holy Grail.

3. ____ Queen Guinevere had a love affair with Sir Mordred.

4. ____ Legends disagree about Arthur's death.

5 Skills in review

Look at the reading *A Busy Day* on p. 18 of the Workbook. It summarizes one person's day. In speech or in writing, summarize your day.

Sentences that DON'T belong in a summary express ideas that are not in the original (see sentence 4 in Exercise 3), too general (see sentence 1), or about small details (see sentence 3).

Vocabulary: Meanings of two-word verbs

Some vocabulary questions on tests focus on two-word verbs that can have more than one meaning. Use the context to decide which meaning is most likely.

1 Understanding two-word verbs in context

Read the e-mail. Circle the letter of the best answer.

1. Verb: *brought up* (paragraph 2)

   Meaning: a. mentioned   b. took care of   c. put in a higher place

2. Verb: *turned into* (paragraph 2)

   Meaning: a. moved   b. changed   c. driven

3. Verb: *draw up* (paragraph 4)

   Meaning: a. pull   b. arrive   c. create

To:	holdenmsa@nddcorp.biz
From:	mccord@nddcorp.biz
Date:	June 13
Subject:	Re: Green Roof

I'd like to follow up on our last meeting about energy policy. We decided to be more active in cutting down our building's use of energy. Of course, we want to save money, but we also want to be good citizens of our community. Using less energy is the right thing to do.

We brought up several ideas for reaching our goal. I'm focusing here on one idea—a "green roof" for our building. This is a good starting point because it can be accomplished quickly and without a lot of expense. The plan is simple. Open areas of the roof will be turned into a garden for local wildflowers, grasses, and small bushes. The plants will keep our building cooler by absorbing sunlight and providing shade. It will have other benefits as well. Less rainwater will run off the roof. Carbon dioxide gas will be used up by the plants, helping—in a very small way—to reduce the warming of our climate.

Here are some concerns: (1) Can our roof hold the extra weight of dirt and plants? (2) Will the roots of the plants damage the roof? (3) Will the green roof attract harmful animals and insects? (4) Will it be hard for us to maintain the new roof? Will we have to hire more maintenance workers? (5) Do local laws restrict the use of green roofs?

As soon as possible, we should hire an architectural consultant to draw up a green roof design and answer these questions. I would be happy to contact several local design firms and ask for bids. Please let me know if you would like me to do this. Thanks.

The basics of a speaking situation

Many questions in listening tests are about the basic situation. Who is speaking? Where are they? Listen for identifiers like *doctor* or *professor*. Also listen for phrases including the words *here* and *this*. They may contain place clues.

Strategies for taking the: **TOEFL® Test**   **TOEIC® Test**   **IELTS™ Test**

2 Who and where

AUDIO FILE 🔊 Listen to Conversation 1. Check (✔) the true statements.

1. ____ The speakers are named Mark and Jenny.

2. ____ They are in Singapore.

3. ____ The two speakers are brother and sister.

4. ____ They are in a classroom.

3 Purposes and problems

AUDIO FILE 🔊 Listen to Conversation 2. Circle the letter of the best answer.

1. Why does Megan go to see Professor James?
   a. To hand in an assignment
   b. To find out what happened in class
   c. To talk about a problem with an assignment

2. Why is Megan worried?
   a. Because her work is too long to fit the assignment
   b. Because she can't finish reading the chapter
   c. Because she doesn't have time to finish writing

3. What does the professor suggest?
   a. Megan should change her report to an outline
   b. Megan should change her outline to a report
   c. Megan should write both an outline and a report

4 Check your understanding

AUDIO FILE 🔊 Listen to Conversation 2 again. Write *T* for true or *F* for false.

1. ____ Megan is a student in the professor's class.

2. ____ Megan read a chapter about a Roman myth.

3. ____ The professor says Megan read the wrong chapter.

4. ____ The professor will let Megan hand in a report instead of an outline.

5 Skills in review

Complete Exercise 11 on p. 27 of the Workbook. Read through your completed interview. Circle all the two-word verbs.

Conversations on English tests often give basic information in the first few sentences. The speakers say each other's names. One speaker may say why he or she wants to speak to the other. Listen for these up-front identifiers.

Unit 5 | Levels of certainty

Some questions on listening tests ask whether a speaker is sure or not. Does he/she think something is *likely*—"almost sure to happen?" Look for verb clues like *will* (likely), *might/could* (possible), or *won't* (not likely).

1 How likely is it?

AUDIO FILE 🔊 Listen to the interview. Circle the best word or phrase.

1. Ann believes another bridge collapse like the Minnesota accident (probably will / probably won't) happen.

2. Ann believes inspectors (will / won't) catch every problem in the state's bridges.

3. Ann says her inspectors (will / might) know if the support under a bridge is getting weaker.

4. Ann is (sure / not sure) that her department will have enough money to inspect bridges properly next year.

2 Why is a speaker sure?

AUDIO FILE 🔊 Listen to the interview again. Match the statement to the reason. Write the letter of the reason.

Statement	Reason why the speaker is sure / not sure
1. ____ A big bridge collapsed in Minnesota.	a. Records contain a list of bridges.
2. ____ There are 1,342 highway bridges in the state.	b. Budget numbers are not yet available.
3. ____ The inspectors caught every big problem with the bridges.	c. The speaker saw pictures from special cameras.
4. ____ The bridge inspectors may or may not have enough money next year.	d. News reports showed it.

Some test questions go beyond "true and false." They offer a third choice—that the reading or listening has *too little* information. Choose this option if you can't tell whether a statement is true or not.

3 Deciding whether a prediction is supported

Read the article. What information can be found in the article? Write *T* if a statement is true according to the article, write *F* if it is false, or write *NI* if there is no information about it in the article.

1. ____ Summer temperatures in the state will probably be warm.

2. ____ Rainy weather will occur at the end of July.

3. ____ This article is mainly about tourism in California.

4. ____ Gasoline prices this summer will be very high.

5. ____ The state mentioned in the article has beaches that tourists visit.

6. ____ Summer workers this year will get higher pay than in most years.

Strategies for taking the: TOEFL® Test   TOEIC® Test   IELTS™ Test

Good Summer Predicted for Tourist Industry

The state's tourist industry will benefit this summer from warm weather and high costs for airline travel. That is the prediction from the State Tourist Board. Hotel and resort owners are hoping those predictions are correct.

The Weather Service says this summer will probably be close to normal, perhaps with an exceptionally warm period at the end of July. That should help draw tourists to the state's beaches and outdoor attractions.

"Normal patterns of high and low pressure will probably be observed this summer. We should see normal summer warmth for most of the season," said Charles Pence, chief forecaster for the Weather Service. "We see a 70 to 80 percent chance that late July will bring a short heat wave, with temperatures five to eight degrees above normal for a week or so."

More people in the state are expected to stay in the state for their vacations this summer, according to the Tourist Board. "Prices for airline tickets are high," said Dora Sundberg, the board's director, "but gas prices are not. This is a good thing for us. Instead of flying to California or Europe, people will drive to vacation spots close to home."

According to Sundberg, almost three-quarters of the money spent on tourism in the state comes from local customers. "We have great beaches, historical destinations, and theme parks," she noted. "Families love us."

State employment officials expect a lot of opportunity in the tourist sector this summer. Hotels, restaurants, and entertainment complexes are already hiring more workers in advance of the strong season. Sundberg said this is good news for students and other seasonal workers. "Any student who wants a summer job in a hotel or restaurant should be able to find one," she said.

4 Check your understanding

Read the article again. Why do speakers mention things? Circle the letter of the best answer.

1. Why does Charles Pence mention "patterns of high and low pressure?"
   a. as problems that could hurt the tourist industry
   b. as things that affect the weather
   c. as reasons why he cannot make exact predictions

2. How does Dora Sundberg describe California and Europe?
   a. as places that sometimes take tourists out of the state
   b. as places that send a lot of tourists to the state
   c. as places that have high gas prices

5 Skills in review

Read *Long Hot Summer...* on p. 30 of the Workbook. Choose three people in the reading and say what their opinions are about the weather. What reasons do they have for their opinions?

Look carefully before choosing a "no information" option. The reading may have the information you need, but in different words. Synonyms—e.g., *employ* for *hire* or *bike* for *bicycle*—may point to the information you need.

Unit 6 | Descriptions

Verbal adjectives -ed and -ing

Many common adjectives are made from verbs like *bore*, *interest*, and *confuse*.
If a class bores students, the class is **boring** and the students are **bored**.
To prepare for test questions about descriptions, practice using -ed and -ing adjectives.

1 Choosing the right adjective

Read the article. Circle the best word.

1. Bethany thinks soccer and music are (interested / interesting).

2. The writer is (troubled / troubling) by the system for educating homeless kids.

3. Kids who have to change schools can feel (threatened / threatening) by a new school.

4. A diet high in sugar and fat is not very (nourished / nourishing).

5. Some children can't sleep well in shelters and are (tired / tiring) all day in school.

Homeless Kids and School

Bethany is 10 years old. She is interested in soccer, music, and riding horses. Bethany is also homeless. Most of our efforts to help the homeless have been very disappointing. The most troubling is our impractical approach to schooling for homeless kids.

In our system, a child goes to a school near his or her home. If you have no fixed home address, you have no permanent school. Bethany's family has moved a lot during the past five years, and she has gone to ten different schools. Many other kids her age complain that elementary school is boring. They wish something new would happen to break up their routine. But new things can be frightening. Kids like Bethany are tired of new schools with strange teachers and unfamiliar classmates. A routine would be comforting. Bethany said she dreams of "saying hi after summer vacation to my teacher and friends from last year."

In school, homeless children often perform poorly. They have a hard time sleeping in temporary shelters. They are tired during the school day and can't concentrate. Also, many homeless children are undernourished. Their families eat poorly, with diets high in sugar and fat and low in nourishing fruits and vegetables. Tired, underfed children are exhausted by the end of the school day. Lessons that might be easy for them if they were healthy just seem long and confusing.

Bethany has an amazing attitude, despite her troubles. "I'm excited about school," she says. "I can't wait to learn new things." Her words are inspiring. Yes, let's learn new things. As a city, let's develop a new educational system for homeless kids. Let's keep them in a single school, long term, even if they move. And let's give them proper food and rest periods once they get to school. We may be amazed by what kids like Bethany could do in a system like that.

Strategies for taking the: TOEFL® Test   TOEIC® Test   IELTS™ Test

2 Practice understanding descriptions

Read the article again. Check (✓) every correct description, according to the article.

1. Bethany is ☐ amazing ☐ confused ☐ inspiring
2. Homeless kids are often ☐ exhausted ☐ undernourished ☐ frightening
3. The city's school policy is ☐ exciting ☐ disappointing ☐ comforting

Wh- questions about descriptions

Some basic information questions on listening tests ask about characteristics. These use question words like *how much*, *what kind*, *how tall*, and *what color*. As you listen, build a picture in your mind of each thing being described.

3 Answering *wh-* questions about characteristics

AUDIO FILE 🔊 Listen to the radio commentary. Circle the letter of the correct answer.

1. How many children does the speaker have?
   a. one   b. two   c. three

2. What kind of day was it?
   a. dark   b. dry   c. cold

3. How old is the speaker?
   a. about 30   b. about 40   c. about 50

4. What color does the speaker mention?
   a. white bread   b. a blue pan   c. black-haired cousins

5. What kind of smell brought memories back to the speaker?
   a. sausage   b. duck   c. pizza

4 Check your understanding

AUDIO FILE 🔊 Listen to the conversation again. Write *T* for true or *F* for false.

1. ____ The speaker and his son were grilling meat in the park.
2. ____ The speaker saw a family preparing to have a meal in the park.
3. ____ The speaker's grandmother spoke Polish.
4. ____ The speaker remembered a Sunday meal at his grandparents' house.

5 Skills in review

Look at Unit 6 in the Workbook. Choose either Kathy Weller (Exercise 6, p. 38) or Sean Matthews (Exercise 7, p. 39). Describe the person you chose. Use at least 5 *-ed* or *-ing* adjectives in your description.

> Pay special attention to questions with *how*. If it's followed by a verb (e.g., *How did you get here?*), it's probably asking about a way or method. If it's followed by an adjective (e.g., *How old is he?*), it's asking for a description.

Unit 7 | Indirect and negative fact questions

Some questions about details are indirect. For example, *Do you know what time it is?* is an indirect way of asking "What time is it?" Focus on the real question. Answer by giving information, not just by saying "yes" or "no."

1 Understanding indirect questions about details

AUDIO FILE 🔊 Listen to the interview. Imagine someone is asking you for information about the interview. Check (✓) the best response.

Questioner: I'd like to know a little bit about the radio interview. Maybe you can help me out. (1) Do you know who Doug and Jenny are?

You: ☐ Yes.   ☐ No.   ☐ Students.

Questioner: (2) Can you see what sports Jenny is interested in?

You: ☐ Yes, I can.   ☐ Running and soccer.   ☐ She isn't.

Questioner: (3) Can you describe Doug?

You: ☐ Mostly in the spring.   ☐ He's a jock.   ☐ They are different.

Questioner: (4) Could you tell me what Doug's idea is?

You: ☐ Yes. Fixing up an old building.   ☐ Yes. A new building.
☐ No. More basketball courts.

Questioner: (5) Do you know how Jenny reacted to that?

You: ☐ Yes, I do.   ☐ Yes. Positively.   ☐ Yes, actually.

Questioner: (6) Can you summarize the difference between their ideas?

You: ☐ She'd prefer a soccer field instead of basketball courts.
☐ She runs cross-country, and he plays lacrosse.
☐ She likes sports, and he doesn't.

2 Word order in indirect questions

AUDIO FILE 🔊 Circle the phrase with the correct word order in each sentence. Then listen to the conversation again and write the answers.

1. Can you tell me (who Doug and Jenny are / who are Doug and Jenny)?

   _____

2. Do you know what they are (about having a discussion / having a discussion about)?

   _____

3. (What could you explain / Could you explain what) Doug's suggestion is?

   _____

4. (You do understand / Do you understand) Jenny's point of view?

   _____

For some test questions, you have to find the answer that is NOT true. These *negative fact* questions are usually multiple choice. The question usually contains the word *NOT* or *EXCEPT*. Notice these words so you understand what to do.

Strategies for taking the: TOEFL® Test   TOEIC® Test   IELTS™ Test

3 Understanding negative fact questions

Read the memo. Circle the letter of the correct answer.

1. Which of the following is NOT a sport mentioned in the memo?

   a. soccer
   b. swimming
   c. lacrosse

2. All of the following are given as reasons for an indoor soccer field EXCEPT

   a. having facilities like other teams
   b. being able to use the field for other sports
   c. being able to play outdoors during the soccer season

3. The memo suggests all the following building projects EXCEPT

   a. a new swimming pool
   b. an arena for horseback riding
   c. better basketball courts

4. According to the memo, all the following college facilities are unsafe EXCEPT

   a. basketball courts
   b. weight rooms
   c. riding arena

To: Dr. David Paine, Director of Construction
From: Chad Foster, Student Council President

Date: November 26

RE: Desirable features for new athletic center

The Camptown Student Council has surveyed students about possible improvements to Camptown's sports facilities. The following is a summary of the suggestions we received.

1. Add an indoor soccer field. Reasons: a) All of the colleges we compete against have indoor soccer fields, so their teams stay in better condition all year round. b) With an indoor field we could have recreational soccer leagues for all students during the winter. c) The field could be used to practice other sports indoors, like lacrosse and field hockey.

2. Put a new surface on our outdoor soccer field. The ground is hard and uneven. This can increase injuries among our players. In many places, the grass has died.

3. Repair and improve our basketball courts. New flooring is needed. Old metal backboards should be replaced with glass. We have enough courts, but they have become unsafe.

4. Create an arena for horseback riding. Camptown has one of the largest riding teams in the United States. We need to build a space for practice and for competitions. Riding arenas are simple to build and are not very costly.

5. Clean and modernize weight-training rooms. We have enough rooms, but the equipment is old and unsafe. Free weights have become rusty, benches are torn, and many machines are broken.

Thank you for your attention. Please contact me if you would like any further information.

---

4 Check your understanding

Read the memo again. Write *T* for true or *F* for false.

1. ____ The writer says many soccer players have been injured on the outdoor field.

2. ____ Some college basketball courts now have bad floors.

3. ____ Currently, Camptown does not have a horseback-riding team.

4. ____ The writer says that the weight-training rooms are clean and modern.

Answer negative fact questions through a "process of elimination." Scan for each option by looking for key words. The option you CAN'T find is the answer. Practice scanning fast so you don't spend too much time on a question.

5 Skills in review

After you fill in the verbs for Exercise 10 on p. 47 of the Workbook, write 3 negative fact questions about the story. For each question, write three answer options—a, b, and c. Two answer options should be true, and one should not be true.

Simplifying sentences

Some test questions focus on the "essential information" in a long sentence. This is its main point without examples or extra details. The answer choices are all simpler than the original sentence. You must find the **simplified** sentence that best gives the essential information.

1 Recognizing simplified sentences

A. Read the article.

How Dogs Became Part of Human Communities

Archaeological evidence shows dogs playing a role in human society for at least 12,000 years. Compare that to other tame animals—cows and sheep for about 10,000 years and horses for less than 5,000. Dogs are by far our oldest companions. How did dogs get to that position? Did they choose us, or did we choose them?

Pet dogs are descended from the wolf. Many biologists believe that dogs split off from the wolf line because humans adopted certain wolves. Eventually, the descendants of these adopted animals came to look very different from wolves, with longer fur, coloring that was usually black and white, brown eyes instead of yellow, and shorter fang teeth. They accepted humans as leaders. Why? Because humans favored such looks and behavior, so animals like this had a greater chance of survival. We made the animals into what we wanted.

Maybe, however, dogs evolved from wolves because of choices that the animals made. Imagine a pack of wolves gathered around the garbage at the edge of a human camp. Almost all the wolves either run away or attack whenever a person comes near, but a few wolves do neither—backing off, but staying nearby.

The humans accept them—after all, they are only eating garbage and are not causing any trouble. This behavior gives those odd, calmer wolves a great survival advantage, because human garbage is a fairly constant and easy-to-get supply of food. These calm wolves mate and have pups that grow up able to live with humans. The development of a companion species is beginning.

When did the split between dog and wolf take place? There is a difference of about one percent between the genome (basic genetic structure) of dogs and that of wolves. At the usual rate of genetic change, then, wolf-dog separation would have happened between 100,000 and 135,000 years ago. That is certainly possible. Other biologists have suggested that the two species split much more recently. Interesting experiments in Siberia that began in 1952 have produced a population of tame foxes—and foxes are similar to dogs and wolves—from wild foxes in only 40 years. If humans did in fact adopt certain wolves as pets, human actions could have pushed the evolution of dogs at a faster pace.

B. Circle the letter of the sentence that best expresses the essential information of the original.

1. Eventually, the descendants of these adopted animals came to look very different from wolves, with longer fur, coloring that was usually black and white, brown eyes instead of yellow, and shorter fang teeth.	2. Almost all the wolves either run away or attack whenever a person comes near, but a few wolves do neither, backing off but staying nearby.	3. Interesting experiments in Siberia that began in 1952 have produced a population of tame foxes—and foxes are similar to dogs and wolves—from wild foxes in only 40 years.
a. Their descendants had more attractive fur, eyes, and teeth.	a. Some animals reacted calmly when humans came by.	a. Foxes in the Siberian experiment are closely related to dogs and wolves.
b. Their descendants differed greatly from wolves.	b. Some animals protected humans from other wolves.	b. Siberian experiments show big changes can happen fast.

Strategies for taking the: TOEFL® Test   TOEIC® Test   IELTS™ Test

2 Understanding numbers in reading

Look again at the article. Circle the best number.

1. Humans and dogs have lived together for at least (12,000 / 135,000) years.

2. Human societies have had horses for about (10,000 / 5,000) years.

3. There is a (1 / 100) percent difference between the basic genetic structure of dogs and wolves.

4. Experiments on Siberian foxes began (in 1952 / 40 years ago).

Understanding numbers: decimals, percentages, fractions

Detail questions on listening tests often ask for accurate understanding of percentages and fractions. The word *percent* is a good listening target. For fractions, listen for *half* or for "ordinal" numbers—two-*thirds*, one-*fourth*, etc.

3 Understanding numbers in listening: fractions and percentages

AUDIO FILE 🔊 Listen to the lecture. Write the letter of the number that best fills each blank in the paragraph. Two numbers will NOT be used.

a. 1/3	b. 1/2	c. 3/5	d. 2/3	e. 2	f. 2.5	g. 3	h. 4	i. 66

Of infants and toddlers, (1) ____ get at least two hours of screen time per day. In other words, about (2) ____ percent of kids aged 0 to (3) ____ get more screen time than the American Academy of Pediatrics recommends. Among kids 8 to 18, the average amount of TV time per day is about (4) ____ hours. In addition, kids get about two hours on computer screens. About (5) ____ of the middle school kids in one Chicago area study had multi-media phones. These kids spent an average of (6) ____ hours per day on their multi-media devices. Screen time could be harmful to kids' health. Kids who got two hours of screen time a day had a (7) ____ greater chance of developing high blood pressure.

4 Check your understanding

AUDIO FILE 🔊 Listen to the lecture again. Write *T* for true or *F* for false.

1. ____ The speaker thinks screen time includes time on multi-media phones.

2. ____ Studies show that teenagers get more screen time than infants / toddlers.

3. ____ The speaker thinks screen time is never good.

4. ____ Screen time is almost all sedentary time.

5 Skills in review

Do Exercise 2 on p. 51 of the Workbook. Listen again to the lecture about screen time. Write at least five *-ing* verb forms that you hear.

To answer *essential information* questions, look at the main clause of a sentence. Also, ignore lists of examples. Most prepositional phrases are also probably not essential information.

Unit 9 | Cause and effect

Causes and effects with conditionals

After a conditional like *If I were* or *If he had*, you might hear about an effect. In this case, the effect is something that was possible but did not actually happen. Listening questions may ask you about these types of effects.

1 Understanding cause-effect situations

AUDIO FILE 🔊 Listen to the press conference. Fill each blank in the table. Use no more than three words for each blank. Listen more than once if necessary.

Cause (real or unreal)	Effect (real or unreal)
1. Because FBI agents _____ 12 people for counterfeiting...	... a shipment of fake $100 bills was stopped.
2. If the fake notes had gone into circulation, ...	... the value of the dollar might have _____.
3. If Agent Hollis were _____ to say how the FBI knew of the operation, ...	... she would tell the reporters.
4. Criminals have access to very good technology, ...	... so they can _____ bills with the 1996 design.
5. Fake U.S. bills are harder to detect outside the U.S, ...	... so the criminals planned to _____ to Asia.

2 Understanding what did / didn't happen

AUDIO FILE 🔊 Listen to the press conference again. Check (✓) each statement that is true according to the listening passage.

1. ☐ The value of the U.S. dollar fell a lot.
2. ☐ The FBI learned of the counterfeiting operation by reading people's e-mail.
3. ☐ Agent Hollis believes a new style of $100 bill is being planned.

Vocabulary: Synonyms

A test question may ask for the word closest in meaning to a *target word* (the word being tested). Sometimes the answer—a **synonym**—is found in the reading. In other cases, you have to depend on your own knowledge of vocabulary. Practice by noticing synonyms as you read or listen.

3 Working with synonyms

Read the article. Match each word on the left with the closest synonym. Write the letter in the blank.

1. ____	circulation	a.	put out
2. ____	currently	b.	bill
3. ____	image	c.	portrait
4. ____	issue	d.	general use
5. ____	note	e.	now

Strategies for taking the: TOEFL® Test   TOEIC® Test   IELTS™ Test

Know Your American Money

- Most U.S. bills have the image of a president (Washington on the $1; Lincoln on the $5). Only two notes in current use show non-presidents— Alexander Hamilton on the $10 bill and Benjamin Franklin on the $100 bill.

- The paper money of the United States is issued by the Federal Reserve Bank, not by the United States Treasury. The Federal Reserve pays the Treasury Department to print the money.

- Now, the highest value of any U.S. paper money is $100. Notes in higher values stopped being printed in 1945 and were officially taken out of circulation in 1969.

- The highest value of any bill is $100,000. A very small number were printed in the 1930s, featuring a portrait of President Woodrow Wilson. They were never actually used by ordinary people, only for exchanges between banks.

- The largest value U.S. banknote ever circulated is the $10,000 bill. It shows a picture of Salmon P. Chase, President Lincoln's Secretary of the Treasury. About 300 of these bills probably still exist. Even though they were declared "not in circulation" in 1969, the government says they still have a value of $10,000 and would be accepted at a government bank. This is unlikely. Because they are so rare, these bills are being held in private money collections. A note in good condition is worth about $500,000 on the collectors' market.

4 Check your understanding

Read the memo again. Write *T* for true or *F* for false.

1. ____ Benjamin Franklin was not a president of the U.S.

2. ____ The U.S. Treasury issues America's paper money.

3. ____ Many ordinary people once used $100,000 bills.

4. ____ If you take a $10,000 bill to a government bank, the bank will accept it.

5 Skills in review

Read the short news stories in Exercise 10 on p. 62 of the Workbook. Find synonyms / near synonyms for: *thief, money, police officer, complained, mistakenly,* and *hurt.*

> In vocabulary questions like *Which word is closest in meaning to X?* be careful. Some answer choices might mean the same as *X* in another context but not in this one. Always find *X* in the reading, and make sure your choice fits into the context before you answer.

Unit 10 | Definitions and expressions of intent or purpose

The answers to some vocabulary questions are given directly in a reading. Phrases like *in other words*, *that is*, or *that means* could introduce a definition. Synonyms may also provide definitions. Understanding these definitions also helps you understand the reading overall.

1 Identifying definitions in a reading

Read the email. Write the letter of the expression that is closest in meaning to the underlined word or phrase.

1. _____ Congress is getting ready to vote on a <u>law</u> called the EVL.	a. a chemical element
2. _____ My new <u>hybrid</u> car gets great gas mileage.	b. bill
3. _____ The batteries use safe lithium <u>compounds</u>.	c. chemical combinations
4. _____ The car batteries won't be useful unless we find a way to <u>recharge</u> them.	d. renew a supply of energy
5. _____ The new batteries contain <u>lithium</u>.	e. using two kinds of engine together

---

To:	Members of EarthPrime
From:	Your EarthPrime leaders
Date:	October 11
Subject:	RE: Contact Congress about Clean Cars

Today is an important turning point in American history. Will you help America turn in the right direction? (1) Congress is considering important legislation to make cars cleaner. (2) This bill, called the "Electric Vehicle Law" (EVL), is meant to provide $700 million for research into new kinds of car batteries. This is the technology of our future. Write to your congressperson to support this important legislation.

(3) The EVL is designed to create a supply of really good lithium-ion batteries for cars. Lithium is a very light metallic element, right after hydrogen and helium on the periodic table. Lithium batteries are extremely common. You probably have one in your laptop computer or maybe even your cell phone. But cars are not computers. A car battery has to survive extreme heat and cold, sudden starts and stops, and demands by power-hungry car parts, from spark plugs to radios. (4) In order to adapt lithium-ion technology to the needs of cars, high-tech laboratory work must continue at major universities throughout the country. The road to the future runs through the research lab.

We have to find better ways to recharge lithium-ion batteries, that is, to renew their supply of electrical energy after long use. (5) For some all-electric cars, recharging would be at plug-in stations, where a driver would pay to hook the car up to an ordinary electrical outlet. We need government support to set up the basics of a national system of plug-in stations. For hybrid cars, those that combine an electric engine with a gasoline-powered engine, research has to make batteries smaller and lighter. Lithium battery packs are highly mutable, meaning they can be made into nearly any shape a car design might require. New chemical compounds—combinations of lithium with manganese, cobalt, and other elements—are safe and environmentally harmless.

Research is needed to push technology ahead, and research takes money. Contact your congressperson today to strengthen America's energy future. Thank you.

Test questions may ask about the purpose of an action. Look for phrases like *designed to*, *supposed to*, *meant to*, or *in order to*. Also, infinitives often have this meaning, as in *I called <u>to ask</u> for a favor.*

2 Practicing with purpose

Read the e-mail again. A number appears before five of the sentences. Write the expression of purpose that you see in each numbered sentence. The first one is done as an example.

1. <u> to make cars cleaner </u>

2. _____

3. _____

4. _____

5. _____

3 Expressions of purpose in speech

AUDIO FILE 🔊 Listen to the conversation. Circle the letter of the best answer.

1. What main task are the students supposed to do in their assignment?
    a. to make a presentation about Mark Twain's writings
    b. to make a presentation about Mark Twain's life
    c. to make a presentation using pictures in a computer slide show

2. What was Jaya's main purpose in reading *Huck Finn*?
    a. to discover Twain's ideas as expressed therein
    b. to finish his work before the others finished theirs
    c. to show that Twain's life was exactly like Huck's

3. What does Jaya mean when he says, "You have to do something else to make it up to me?"
    a. The others have to explain the project to him.
    b. The others have to do other work that is equal to what he did.
    c. The others have to tell the teacher that Jaya did an excellent job.

4 Check your understanding

AUDIO FILE 🔊 Listen to the conversation again. Write *T* for true or *F* for false.

1. ____ A book known as *Huck Finn* was written by Mark Twain.

2. ____ Jaya, Mariana, and Omar will do a presentation together.

3. ____ Jaya is the only one who is reading *Huck Finn*.

4. ____ Mark Twain was poor and illiterate.

5 Skills in review

Read the article about laptops on p. 64 of the Workbook. Find expressions of intent that include *aim, designed,* and *so*. What intent is expressed in each one? (Be careful. *Designed* and *so* also appear in sentences that do not show intent.)

Definitions in a reading might be found in parentheses, "( )", dashes, "–", or commas. You can easily scan for these.

Unit 11 | Doubts and inferences

Some test questions ask whether a speaker does or doesn't believe that something is true. A speaker who *doubts* (doesn't believe) something may ask questions about it. Some expressions of doubt are *really?*, *it can't be*, or *you don't mean*.

1 Understanding a speaker's doubts

AUDIO FILE 🔊 Listen to the questioning by the police officer. Put a check (✓) next to the things the officer believes, and an X next to things he doubts.

1. ____ There was an accident at the beach.

2. ____ The injured man was swimming.

3. ____ The injured man was in the water.

4. ____ A kid on a surfboard hit the injured man.

5. ____ The injured man shouted for help.

6. ____ The two witnesses are unreliable.

Making inferences

To fully understand a reading or listening passage, you might have to "read between the lines." Some test questions ask you to make *inferences*—to understand something that is not said directly. Use clues from the information that IS given. Also use logic and your own experience.

2 Inferring from clues in a text

AUDIO FILE 🔊 Listen again to the questioning by the police officer. How strongly can you infer each idea? "Strong" = strongly inferred; "Maybe" = possibly inferred; "No"= not inferred.

1. _____ The police officer and witnesses are at a beach.

2. _____ Someone has died in an accident at the beach.

3. _____ The police officer trusts the woman's statements more than the man's.

4. _____ Next, the police officer will interview the kid.

3 Practice making inferences

Read the article. Circle the letter of the best answer.

1. The police stopped Gordon Simcoe because
   a. he did not have a driver's license.
   b. he broke a traffic law.
   c. he was using a fake identity.

2. At the time the article was written, Gordon Simcoe was
   a. at home.
   b. in Mississippi.
   c. in jail.

3. It is most likely that, at the time he disappeared, Gordon VanDriel did not want to
   a. get married.
   b. go boating.
   c. work with computers.

4. Gordon Simcoe most probably told officers about his other identity because
   a. they forced him to.
   b. they already knew about it.
   c. he wanted to stop living a secret life.

Strategies for taking the: (TOEFL® Test)   (TOEIC® Test)   (IELTS™ Test)

Traffic Stop Nets Man "Dead" for 27 Years

Pigeon Forge, TN

A routine traffic stop here resulted in the arrest of a man who supposedly died almost three decades ago. Gordon Simcoe of Knoxville was detained in the Knox County jail on charges of making false statements to police and resisting arrest.

The sheriff's office reported that Simcoe was stopped at approximately 11:25 p.m. He refused to answer officers' questions and would not produce a driver's license. He was then arrested and questioned at the County Municipal Building. After identifying himself as Gordon Simcoe of Knoxville, he volunteered that *Simcoe* is an assumed name. He claimed that his real name is Gordon VanDriel and said he was born in Gulfport, Mississippi.

Officials are investigating the possibility that Simcoe is a man presumed dead in a boating accident 27 years ago. At that time, a 22-year-old Gulfport resident named Gordon VanDriel disappeared while sailing in the Gulf of Mexico. Wreckage of his small boat was found about a mile from shore, but no body was ever found. A year later, a court declared that VanDriel had died accidentally.

Records indicate that Gordon Simcoe owns a computer-services company, Gordon's Data Services, in Knoxville. Simcoe said he lives in Knoxville with his wife and two children. Sheriff's officials said they were unsure why Simcoe then told them about being VanDriel.

Simcoe said that, as Gordon VanDriel, he had graduated from Camptown College in Florida with a degree in engineering. At the time of his presumed accident, he was working with a computer-services company in Gulfport and was engaged to be married. He told officers that in his 20s, he had felt trapped and dissatisfied. He said he had faked the boating accident so he could disappear and start a new life.

No details were available of how Simcoe/VanDriel might have established a new identity. Experts with the Tennessee State Police said a false identity, including a new social security number and identity papers, is nearly impossible to set up. However, Fred Abner, a private security expert, said the police exaggerate this difficulty. "Give me fifteen minutes and access to county records," Abner said, "and I can walk away with a totally new life. It's just a matter of being smart."

4 Check your understanding

Read the memo again. Write *T* for true or *F* for false.

1. ____ Gordon Simcoe has a family in Knoxville.

2. ____ If Simcoe is VanDriel, he is 49 years old.

3. ____ Simcoe now lives in Gulfport.

4. ____ Experts all agree that setting up a new identity is impossible.

5 Skills in review

Look again at the pictures on pp. 72–73 of the Workbook. What else can you infer from them? Make at least one more inference about each one.

> Follow the evidence! The answer to an inference question always relates to information in the reading or listening. If you can't find evidence, don't choose an answer.

Details of personal impressions

A writer's personal impressions can be very specific—much more than "positive" or "negative." Test questions may ask for details about these impressions. Look for opinion-related adjectives (e.g., *crowded*, *old-fashioned*) or noun phrases (e.g., *sophisticated technology*).

1 Understanding personal impressions

Read the blog entries. Which statements correctly tell the writer's opinions? Write *T* for true or *F* for false.

1. ____ The surface of the track hurts a runner's knees.

2. ____ To safely lift weights, a person has to know about the body's muscles.

3. ____ Personal trainers charge too much money.

4. ____ The houses and gardens in the writer's neighborhood are well cared for.

5. ____ People born on February 29 get too many birthday presents.

ℹ Internet Search   _ □ x

Address `http://kylepeters.myblog.com` ▼ Go

Posted by KylePeters 17:43 EST on Friday February 27

Today I joined a health club. Finally, after years of being out of shape, I'm going to get healthy. Worked out for about 2 hours. First, I ran for half an hour on a track inside the building. Nice track, with a soft rubber-like surface. No knee pain. But running around and around on a track is really boring. Next time, I have to bring a music player. After running, I lifted weights. Ouch! I think I know too little about muscle groups in the body. Maybe I should get advice from a professional trainer, so I don't hurt myself.

Posted by KylePeters 09:12 EST on Saturday February 28

I am sooooo sore! I think I overdid it with the exercise yesterday. This will be a rest day. I'm sure glad it's Saturday, so no one at work can see how sore I am. About getting a personal trainer... I called a couple of trainers yesterday to find out how much they charged. Yikes! There's NO way I can afford that. They are extremely expensive, probably meant for serious athletes, not for ordinary guys like me.

Posted by KylePeters 20:21 EST on Saturday February 28

Spent most of the day on the couch watching TV. I was going crazy. I had to get out of the house! I took my dog Scout for a very slow walk through the neighborhood. As Scout and I shuffled along, I noticed things I usually pass quickly by—a nice garden, lots of things. If you look carefully enough, you see that people around here take very good care of their property.

Posted by KylePeters 17:43 EST on Sunday February 29

Leap Day! It must be weird to have your birthday on February 29. Does that mean you have a birthday only once every four years? Just kidding. I know you celebrate it on February 28, although I suppose you could celebrate it on March 1 instead. I really feel sorry for people whose birthday is some big holiday like December 25 or July 4. People probably just forget about your birthday, and you don't get as many presents. I decided to go back to the health club today, even though I'm really stiff and sore. You have to play through the pain, right?

Strategies for taking the: (**TOEFL® Test**)   (**TOEIC® Test**)   (**IELTS™ Test**)

Some tests ask about the relationships among details in a reading or listening passage. Do the details fit into categories? Which idea does each one support?

2 Relating details to larger ideas

Read the blog entries again. Write the letter of the idea that each detail supports.

> IDEAS: a. Personal trainers are expensive.
>   b. Running on a track is boring.
>   c. Walking slowly helps you appreciate things around you.

1. ____ **Detail:** The music player

2. ____ **Detail:** Serious athletes

3. ____ **Detail:** The garden

3 Connecting information to complete a chart

AUDIO FILE 🔊 Listen to the lecture. Complete the chart by checking (✓) the correct boxes. For some ideas, more than one box should be checked.

IDEA / DETAIL	Early times	The 1600s	The 1700s
1. A column of mercury			
2. Air is a basic element.			
3. Air is made up of many parts.			
4. Air is nothing but the empty space between objects.			
5. Air puts pressure on things.			
6. Lavoisier			
7. Magdeburg spheres			
8. phlogiston			
9. Plato			
10. Priestley			

4 Check your understanding

AUDIO FILE 🔊 Listen again to the lecture. Write *T* for true or *F* for false.

1. ____ Plato and other early thinkers performed scientific experiments on air.

2. ____ In a vacuum, there is no air.

3. ____ Benjamin Franklin is often credited with discovering oxygen.

> A speaker might give structure clues that connect information. Listen for listing expressions like *one result...* or *another technique...* .

5 Skills in review

Read the article on p. 77 of the Workbook. Do you have positive or negative impressions of Mrs. Small and Mr. Flashman? Why do you feel like you do? Give specific reasons.

Answer Key

Unit 1 (pp. 2–3)
1 **Listening for details about differences** A: 1. F; 2. T; 3. F; 4. T; 5. F. **B:** 1. b; 2. b; 3. c
2 *Wh-* **questions related to differences** 1. a; 2. b; 3. a
3 **Finding answers to** *wh-* **questions about differences** 1. a; 2. b; 3. b; 4. b; 5. a
4 **Check your understanding** 1. F; 2. T; 3. T; 4. T
5 **Skills in review** Answers will vary.

Unit 2 (pp. 4–5)
1 **Understanding usual and current actions** 1. U; 2. N; 3. N; 4. U; 5. U; 6. N
2 **Active and passive verbs in the present** Check 2
3 **Choosing verb forms** 1. b; 2. b; 3. a; 4. d
4 **Check your understanding** 1. F; 2. T; 3. F; 4. T
5 **Skills in review** Answers will vary.

Unit 3 (pp. 6–7)
1 **Listening for where and when** 1. Germany; 2. Iowa; 3. 1859; 4. a shared kitchen; 5. Amana Society, Inc.; 6. 1934
2 **Summarizing a narrative** 1. moved; 2. beliefs; 3. share; 4. together; 5. private
3 **Prose Summary** Check 2, 5, 6
4 **Check your understanding** 1. T; 2. T; 3. F; 4. T
5 **Skills in review** Answers will vary.

Unit 4 (pp. 8–9)
1 **Understanding two-word verbs in context** 1. a; 2. b; 3. c
2 **Who and where** Check 1, 4
3 **Purposes and problems** 1. c; 2. a; 3. a
4 **Check your understanding** 1. T; 2. T; 3. F; 4. F
5 **Skills in review** Answers will vary.

Unit 5 (pp. 10–11)
1 **How likely is it?** 1. probably won't; 2. won't; 3. will; 4. not sure
2 **Why is a speaker sure?** 1. d; 2. a; 3. c; 4. b
3 **Deciding whether a prediction is supported** 1. T; 2. F; 3. F; 4. F; 5. T; 6. F
4 **Check your understanding** 1. b; 2. a
5 **Skills in review** Answers will vary.

Unit 6 (pp. 12–13)
1 **Choosing the right adjective** 1. interesting; 2. troubled; 3. threatened; 4. nourishing; 5. tired
2 **Practice understanding descriptions** 1. amazing, inspiring; 2. exhausted, undernourished; 3. disappointing
3 **Answering wh- questions about characteristics** 1. a; 2. b; 3. b; 4. b; 5. a
4 **Check your understanding** 1. F; 2. T; 3. T; 4. T
5 **Skills in review** Answers will vary.

Unit 7 (pp. 14–15)

1 **Understanding indirect questions about details** 1. Students; 2. Running and soccer; 3. He's a jock.; 4. Yes. Fixing up an old building; 5. Yes, positively.; 6. She'd prefer a soccer field instead of basketball courts.

2 **Word order in indirect questions** 1. who Doug and Jenny are; 2. having a discussion about; 3. Could you explain what; 4. Do you understand

3 **Understanding negative fact questions** 1. b; 2. c; 3. a; 4. c

4 **Check your understanding** 1. F; 2. T; 3. F; 4. F

5 **Skills in review** Answers will vary.

Unit 8 (pp. 16–17)

1 **Recognizing simplified sentences** 1. a; 2. a; 3. b

2 **Understanding numbers in reading** 1. 12,000; 2. 5,000; 3. 1; 4. in 1952

3 **Understanding numbers in listening: fractions and percentages** 1. d; 2. i; 3. g; 4. h; 5. c; 6. f; 7. a

4 **Check your understanding** 1. T; 2. T; 3. F; 4. T

5 **Skills in review** Answers will vary.

Unit 9 (pp. 18–19)

1 **Understanding cause-effect situations** 1. arrested; 2. fallen; 3. able; 4. copy; 5. ship them

2 **Understanding what did / didn't happen** Check 3

3 **Working with synonyms** 1. d; 2. e; 3. c; 4. a; 5. b

4 **Check your understanding** 1. T; 2. F; 3. F; 4. T

5 **Skills in review** Answers will vary.

Unit 10 (pp. 20–21)

1 **Identifying definitions in a reading** 1. b; 2. e; 3. c; 4. d; 5. a

2 **Practicing with purpose** 2. to provide $700 million (for research); 3. to create a supply (of really good lithium-ion batteries for cars); 4. to adapt lithium-ion technology (to the needs of cars); 5. to hook the car up (to an ordinary electrical outlet)

3 **Expressions of purpose in speech** 1. b; 2. a; 3. b

4 **Check your understanding** 1. T; 2. T; 3. T; 4. F

5 **Skills in review** Answers will vary.

Unit 11 (pp. 22–23)

1 **Understanding a speaker's doubts** 1. ✓; 2. X; 3. X; 4. X; 5. ✓; 6. ✓

2 **Inferring from clues in a text** 1. Strong; 2. No; 3. No; 4. Maybe

3 **Practice making inferences** 1. b; 2. c; 3. a; 4. c

4 **Check your understanding** 1. T; 2. T; 3. F; 4. F

5 **Skills in review** Answers will vary.

Unit 12 (pp. 24–25)

1 **Understanding personal impressions** 1. F; 2. T; 3. T; 4. T; 5. F

2 **Relating details to larger ideas** 1. b; 2. a; 3. c

3 **Connecting information to complete a chart** Early times: 2, 4, 9; The 1600s: 1, 5, 7; The 1700s: 3, 6, 8, 10

4 **Check your understanding** 1. F; 2. T; 3. F

5 **Skills in review** Answers will vary.

Audio Scripts

Unit 1

I = Interviewer   T = Tom

I: Our guest today is a senior here at Camptown College. Tom Sutton comes from Montana….

T: Hi.

I: Hi, Tom. And we're going to talk about lifestyles. Tom, was it a big shock to come from Montana to a college in Florida?

T: Absolutely. I like it here, but I just can't do a lot of my favorite things.

I: Oh, really?

T: Like hiking. In Montana, I hike through the mountains a lot, but here everything is pretty flat.

I: Yes, that's true. But people go hiking in Florida, too.

T: True, but here… I don't know… the world seems smaller. Montana is very open. When you're hiking, you can see for miles and miles.

I: Any other differences?

T: In Florida, I think you see your neighbors more than we do in Montana. People live a lot closer together here. My closest neighbors back home live about a half mile away.

I: I see. How about fun? What do kids in Montana do?

T: Some of the things are the same as here, like online games and soccer. But my friends and I do a lot of riding, too—I mean on horses.

I: There are a lot of horses around here, too.

T: Yeah, I know. A few people ride. But in my town almost everyone has at least one horse.

I: And the weather?

T: Well, sure. Big differences. We have hot summers back home, just like here, but the winters are really cold.

I: So, Florida is better.

T: [chuckles] I didn't say THAT. I like winter. And I have to say, the air in Florida is always too humid for me. I like dry air, like we have in Montana.

I: Thanks, Tom.

T: My pleasure.

Unit 2

Student Employment Opportunities

Professor (female): I'm so glad to see so many new students here at today's orientation session. Students often ask me, "How can I earn some money while I study?" Are any of you wondering the same thing? Yes, I see. At least half of you are holding up your hands. I usually answer that question with another question, "What do you like to do?"

I say that because students at this college are given many, many job opportunities. Some students help out in the library. Others clean college buildings. Others do office work in the administration building. I am listing only some of the most common jobs, the ones that are usually found on the "Student Employment" page at our Human Resources Web site. These are college jobs. You are hired by the college as a whole. But in my little talk today, I am trying to show you some other possibilities.

Let me first give you some statistics. About forty percent of the student jobs on campus are not listed on the Human Resources Web site. Forty percent. That's about four hundred eighty jobs. Students find out about them by asking individual departments.

This semester, more than eighty students are working in biology labs on campus. These students are hired by the Biology department, not by the college. New research projects are approved every semester. Most of these need student workers.

So what am I trying to say? Explore! Great jobs are being offered in many places. Now, at the start of a new semester, is the best time to find a job. Departments are looking especially hard for workers.

Unit 3

Lecturer: Today we will talk about one of the most successful community-living efforts in American history, the Amana Colonies. They are located in east-central Iowa, in the American Midwest. Seven small towns and the farmland around them, make up the colonies.

In 1842 and 1843, a religious group called the Community of True Inspiration moved from Germany to America, so they could more freely live according to their beliefs. First, the Inspirationists lived near Buffalo, New York. Then, in 1859, looking for more room, they bought farmland at their present location near the Iowa River.

Inspirationists believed that a community should work together and share what they own. That's how life in Amana was organized. Elected leaders decided where people lived and worked. Each family was assigned a house, but they ate their daily meals with other nearby families in a shared kitchen. The land was owned by everyone. Neighbors worked together to raise crops, educate their children, and keep the community running. Any money from selling their crops or other products was shared by the whole community. The community treated outside visitors kindly, but they tried to keep separate from the outside world. They emphasized their separateness by speaking German, not English, within Amana.

By the early 1930s, many Inspirationists wanted a more modern life, including pleasures like baseball and radio programs. In 1932, the people of Amana voted for "the Great Change." Their church stayed together, so the community did not fall apart, but their economy changed. A private company, the Amana Society, Inc., took over the ownership of farms and shops. Its goal was to make a profit, not to improve community life. Inspirationists got shares in the company, but they were free to sell their shares if they liked. They could also set up new businesses. In 1934, George Foerstner started Amana Refrigeration, Inc. Originally operated by the Amana Society, it became one of America's largest producers of refrigerators and other kitchen appliances in the United States. Most of Amana's business was bought in 2006 by the Whirlpool Corporation.

Unit 4A

Conversation 1

M = Mark   J = Jenny

M: Hi, Jenny. It's nice to be back here at school, isn't it?

J: [laughs a little] Yeah. Hi, Mark. How are you?

M: Oh, fine. I just wish summer vacation could have lasted longer.

J: Really? Did you go anywhere?

M: Yes, I did. I spent three weeks in Singapore visiting my sister.

J: Incredible! I've been to Singapore too!

M: Woah! I didn't know that. When were you there?

J: Last winter. I went with a group from my political science class.

M: My sister works for a bank there, so I went and stayed with her. I really liked it.

J: When I went, we spent most of our time downtown—the parliament building, the courts, that kind of thing.

M: I didn't go to those things. Just to the zoo, and the beach, and a bunch of restaurants.

J: [whispers] Okay. Class is starting. Let's talk more later.

Unit 4B
Conversation 2

M = Megan   PJ = Professor James

M: Hi, Professor. Do you have a minute?

PJ: Sure, Megan. How can I help you?

M: I've just been trying to finish our assignment about Roman myths, and I'm not sure I understand what to do.

PJ: Okay. What's the problem?

M: Well, so I read the chapter about Hercules, and I started writing my report.

PJ: Good.

M: But the assignment says I can't write any more than two pages, and my report is six pages long! I don't know how to make it shorter.

PJ: Hmmm. You said "report?" You know, the assignment asks for an outline, not a report.

M: An outline?

PJ: Yes. An outline. A, B, C, 1, 2, 3. Like that. Not full sentences.

M: Oh. I see the problem. I guess I didn't read it carefully. All that writing for nothing!

PJ: Just shorten it up so it's an outline, Megan. It's not really a waste. Think about how well you understand Hercules now!

Unit 5

D = Dan   M = Marta

D: Hi. This is Dan Phillips, and we're talking today about bridges on our highways. Are they safe? My guest is Marta Delgado, chief engineer for the state highway department. Welcome, Marta.

M: Hi, Dan. Thanks for having me.

D: Marta, a few years ago we all saw news reports that a big highway bridge collapsed in Minnesota. Several people died. Is that likely to happen again?

M: Let me just say, Dan, that another big bridge collapse like that is very, very unlikely. It is even less likely since the Minnesota accident. Bridges are inspected much more often now.

D: That's good to hear, but there are so many bridges. Safety inspectors can't possibly spot every problem.

M: True. Our inspectors can't catch every problem, but we do catch the big ones. Our records show that in our state, there are one thousand three hundred forty-three bridges on state or federal highways.

D: That's a huge number!

M: Yes, but you would be surprised how much attention each one gets. Last year, our department did at least one major structural inspection of every bridge.

D: That's more than a hundred bridges a month. Are you sure you caught all of the problems? What if you missed something?

M: We used special X-ray cameras to look at the basic structure of every bridge. I saw the pictures of most of those. I believe we caught every BIG problem. Not every tiny thing, but….

D: So, did you find problems?

M: Sure. With that many bridges, some problems had to exist. We closed nine bridges for a short time while we made repairs.

D: What were some common problems?

M: Well, the big problems involved the metal supports under the bridges. Metal rusts and gets weaker.

D: How can you tell if a bridge has weak supports? Do you have to drive heavy things over it?

M: [laughs] No, no. We use those special cameras and chemical tests. If a bridge support is getting weak, we know it.

D: Marta, we all know that government spending is going down. How can you take care of the bridges if you don't have enough money?

M: Our bridge inspection budget for this year is the same as last year. We have enough money to do our job this year. Next year could be a different story. I haven't seen any budget numbers yet.

D: Thanks very much, Marta.

M: Thank you for having me on the program, Dan.

Unit 6

Commentator: A familiar smell can bring childhood memories suddenly into focus. That happened to me two weeks ago—a sudden, surprising trip back to 30 years ago. I was walking with my son through the park. We fed the ducks on a little pond, and then we walked toward the playground. The sky was dry and blue. A soft warm breeze carried sounds and smells through the rosebushes, over the bright green grass, and around the black trunks of oak trees. About 50 yards away, a large family had spread food out along two picnic tables. Bright white tablecloths flapped under bowls of salad, baskets of bread, bottles of water, and bags of potato chips. Two of the men in the family were barbecuing smoky meat on a park grill.

Then it struck me. As my little boy ran ahead of me, I stopped to smell the sausage. I closed my eyes, and suddenly I was 10 years old again, in my grandmother's kitchen on an autumn Sunday. Coils of Polish sausage roasted to a crust in a dark-blue pan. My grandmother said something in Polish, a language I didn't understand, and my father started chopping cabbage for a salad. Fresh brown rye bread was just coming out of the extra oven in the basement. My red-haired younger cousins ran through the kitchen and into the dining room, where my Aunt Ginny grabbed them and told them to sit nicely at the table.

"Dad!" said my son Tyler as he tackled my leg, and I was jolted back to the present. The sausages on the grill were nearly done. At least, that's what I think the two grilling men said to each other, in a language I thought must be Polish, or Ukrainian, or some sister tongue. Just like my Polish grandparents, they were bringing old-country cooking to the American Midwest. Their family gathered, like mine used to, around garlicky-sweet foods born in Eastern Europe and told their children to sit nicely at the table to enjoy them. I knew my son and I would probably have some pizza when we got home from the park. I think maybe we have lost something.

Unit 7

I = Interviewer   J = Jenny   D = Doug

I: Hi, everyone. Today we're having a discussion about campus sports. I'm talking to two Camptown College students, Jenny Evans…

J: Hi.

I: …and Doug Johnson.

D: How's it goin'?

I: So, Jenny, can you tell us what sports you're interested in?

J: I love soccer but just for fun. I can't make a big time commitment to it. Too much studying! But I do run cross-country on our varsity team.

D: In the spring I play varsity lacrosse. But all year round I do weight-training, basketball, lots of stuff. I guess I'm a jock.
[all laugh a little]

I: Can I ask—Doug, let's turn to you. Can I ask what Camptown should do better in terms of sports facilities? What don't we have?

D: We have a real big need for more basketball courts. During the winter, that's like the most popular sport.

J: I like basketball, too, but we already have six courts. We have absolutely NO indoor soccer field.

I: Interesting. Those are two big things. Does anyone know what a basketball court or a soccer field costs?

J: I'm sure it's millions. You'd have to put up a whole new building.

D: Well, it wouldn't be cheap, but I think we could do it without a new building.

I: Uh…okay…can you say more about that?

D: You know that big storage building by the gym? You could like fix that place up. It's big enough to put in a couple of basketball courts, locker rooms, and everything.

J: Actually, that's not a bad idea. Fix that place up. But a soccer field would be better in there. Basketball courts are made of wood and you need better heat. A soccer field can take cold and moisture and all that.

D: Well, I don't….

I: I'm sorry, guys, but our time is up. My thanks to Doug and Jenny. Great ideas.

Unit 8

Professor: Parents in the 21st century have to worry about a thing called "screen time"—the amount of time a child spends looking at a screen. This could be a TV screen, a computer monitor, or the screen on a multimedia phone. Different studies of kids' behavior find different figures, but here are some representative numbers.

The Kaiser Family Foundation[1] found that two-thirds of infants and toddlers watch a screen about 2 hours a day. These are young kids—three years old or younger. So you've got about 66 percent of, say, two year-olds parked in front of a screen. At this age it's usually a TV because most little kids don't really operate computers. Just for your information, the American Academy of Pediatrics recommends no more than two hours of screen time each day for any kid. But then you've got kids and teens 8 to 18 years spending nearly 4 hours a day in front of a TV screen and almost 2 hours beyond that on computers or playing video games. And I mean computers outside school and not involving homework. My own research adds to this. The Kaiser numbers came from a time before a lot of kids had multi-media phones and music players. I did a study last year in three Chicago suburbs tracking how much time middle-school kids spend on these devices. I found that the average middle-school kid with a multi-media phone spends about two-and-a-half hours on it each day. Some of that time is during school hours because they play games and text each other when teachers aren't looking. Oh, and I should mention that about three-fifths of the kids at these suburban schools do have multi-media phones. More than half.

I don't want to say that screen time is all bad. After all, these kids will grow into a job market that requires screen time. However, there is evidence that too much of it can be bad for kids' health. One study in Michigan showed that 2 hours of screen time a day gave kids a one-third greater chance of high blood pressure problems. Of course, there's the problem of kids being overweight. Slightly less than 20 percent of middle school kids are now considered obese, and sedentary—"sitting-down"— activity promotes excess body weight. Screen time is almost 100 percent sedentary.

Unit 9

NS = Nancy Hollis
Reporters: JB = Jeff Baker   FJ = Faye Jameson
            CS = Carter Stone   MC = Mariana Cannon

NH: Ladies and gentlemen of the press, thank you for coming. I have some prepared comments, and then I will take questions. Yesterday, the Federal Bureau of Investigation—the FBI—arrested 12 people in New Jersey and charged them with counterfeiting U.S. currency. This operation also involved New Jersey State Police officers based in Newark. We believe these arrests have broken up the largest counterfeiting operation on U.S. soil in the past 50 years. I will now take questions…. Yes, over there.

JB: Jeff Baker, FBC News. Agent Hollis, what do you think would have happened if the FBI had not broken up this operation?

NH: We believe the suspects were preparing to ship at least 15 million dollars in fake 100-dollar bills to associates in East Asia. If we had not interfered, we believe this would have happened soon. Yes?

FJ: Faye Jameson, New York News. What if the shipment had succeeded?

NH: An amount that large can cause major economic problems. As the fake bills started circulating, the value of the dollar might have fallen quite a bit.

CS: Carter Stone, Metro News. How did the FBI learn about this counterfeiting?

NH: I am not free to give out any information about that.

CS: Was it a tip from the public? Did the FBI intercept phone conversations, or e-mail, or…

NH: If I were able to tell you, I would. However, those details cannot be made public. Anyone else?

MC: Mariana Cannon, Weekly Magazine. So, is this a sign that American money is too easy to copy? Should the Federal Reserve change the look of our currency?

NH: I'm no currency expert, but I think a new design is already planned. If hundred-dollar bills had more high-tech security features, maybe criminals would have a harder time copying them. The fake bills we found use the 1996 design. That design is good, but counterfeiters now have the technology to copy it. I think new 100s are coming out soon…. OK, one more question…. Yes, Mr. Baker again.

JB: You said these fakes were being shipped to Asia. Why?

NH: Well, of course, U.S. currency is used in transactions all around the world. If the criminals had released so many new bills into the U.S. economy, they would

1. KidsHealth, "How TV Affects Your Child," The Nemours Foundation 2009. Accessed August 2009 at http://kidshealth.org/parent/positive/family/tv_affects_child.html.

have been more easily discovered. But if they had spread these bills throughout the world—China, India, Africa, wherever—they could have gone years without detection. Okay. That's all. Thank you very much.

Unit 10

J = Jaya   M = Mariana   O = Omar

J: Hi, Mariana. Hi, Omar. I'm almost done reading *Huck Finn*. How about you?

M: Hi, Jaya. Reading *Huck Finn*? Why are you doing that? We're supposed to talk about Mark Twain's life, not about the books.

O: I haven't read it. Do we have to?

J: Well, you can't really answer questions about Twain's life unless you read it. It's almost like a map of Twain's way of thinking. In order to know where his personal thoughts came from, you have to know about Huck.

M: Oh, come on, Jaya. Twain was rich and cultured and hung around with famous people. He wasn't at all like Huck. Huck Finn was an illiterate kid and didn't have any money and…

O: But Jaya does have a point. The assignment says, "Explore Twain's social and political views." Don't we have to read his works in order to do that?

J: Well, anyway, I'm reading it, so I can say something about how it relates to Twain's life. You guys don't really have to read it. But this is meant to be an equal assignment. You have to do something else to make it up to me. I did my share, now you do yours.

M: Well, the main thing is to plan out our presentation. Fifteen minutes. That's a long time. To keep people interested for fifteen minutes, we have to have pictures and handouts and all sorts of things.

J: Okay, to keep the workload fair, you guys find all the pictures.

O: Pictures. Well, that means doing a slide show on the computer. Will we have a projector in the room?

J: I think we're supposed to contact the media service people to order one.

Unit 11

N = Narrator   I = Investigator
MW = Male witness   FW = Female witness

N: A police investigator is interviewing two witnesses to an accident at a beach.

[male and female witnesses are speaking excitedly]

I: I have to ask you both some questions about the injuries to Mr. Johnson. So, you said Mr. Johnson was swimming far from shore…

MW: That's right. Maybe about 150 yards out there.

FW: No. He wasn't swimming. He was walking. Like walking slowly through the waves.

I: Well, was he carrying anything?

MW: Yeah. He had a lunchbox in his hands, something like a little cooler for drinks.

I: Really? How could he swim if he was carrying that?

FW: It's like I said. He was walking. And then this kid came riding by on a surfboard and just hit him.

I: Kid? What kid?

MW: There wasn't any kid. He was swimming and then this big wave knocked him out.

FW: I didn't see any wave. It was some kid surfing by really fast and then….Maybe that's him over there, in the red swimsuit.

I: But if there weren't any waves, how could the kid be riding a surfboard?

FW: Not riding it, I guess. Maybe more like paddling it. It's him. It's that kid over there.

I: Look, I need you both to calm down. Take a deep breath. Think about what you really saw.

MW: I know what I saw. The guy was swimming, and then a big wave came, and then he started shouting for help.

I: You don't really mean he started shouting, do you? He was unconscious, right? Knocked out?

FW: Yeah. Like I said. Knocked out by some kid on a surfboard. Bam!

I: Okay. Thank you. I'll call you if I need more information.

MW: Wait. I didn't get a chance to tell you about the shark…..

Unit 12

Lecturer: Today let's talk about how scientists became interested in air. I mean in what air is. Of course, early thinkers like Plato considered it one of the basic elements—you know, earth, air, fire, and water. But they didn't do much real science related to air. A lot of other early thinkers didn't believe air was anything at all. In fact, air was often considered a sort of nothing, just the space between so-called "real" things like trees and people. Unless air was full of something, like smoke or disease or evil spirits, many people were not interested in it.

In Europe during the 1600s, some interesting creations showed very clearly that air had weight. Specifically, they showed that air could put pressure on things. An Italian scientist named Evangelista Torricelli showed that air pressure made a column of mercury—a silvery liquid metal—go up and down in a glass tube. Then in 1654, a German, Otto von Guericke, put on a great demonstration in the city of Magdeburg. First, he took two hemispheres, like the two sides of a tennis ball that had been cut in half. After fitting them together, he used a strong machine to suck out all the air inside—to create a vacuum. He then got two teams of 15 horses each. Each team was hooked up to one hemisphere, and each tried pulling away from the other. Air pushing on the outside of this "Magdeburg Sphere" was so strong that not even these horses could pull the hemispheres apart.

Then, some really serious study of air's parts took place in the 1700s. Joseph Priestley—a British scientist who was close friends with Benjamin Franklin—is often credited with discovering that oxygen is part of air. Not exactly. Priestley did experiments placing animals and plants inside containers of air. He discovered that a candle's flame or the breathing of animals took something out of air that a mint plant apparently put back. So he DID systematically show that ordinary air is made up of different gases. Actually, though, the French chemist Antoine de Lavoisier thought more clearly about air. He first named oxygen and hydrogen and pointed out that they were chemicals. He popularized the idea that when things burned or rusted, they used oxygen from the air. Priestley, on the other hand, believed in a mysterious substance called phlogiston that helped things burn or rust—an idea left over from the 1600s. Lavoisier moved beyond phlogiston to modern ideas about chemical elements.

OXFORD
UNIVERSITY PRESS

198 Madison Avenue
New York, NY 10016 USA

Great Clarendon Street, Oxford ox2 6dp UK

Oxford University Press is a department of the University of Oxford.
It furthers the University's objective of excellence in research, scholarship,
and education by publishing worldwide in

Oxford   New York

Auckland   Cape Town   Dar es Salaam   Hong Kong   Karachi
Kuala Lumpur   Madrid   Melbourne   Mexico City   Nairobi
New Delhi   Shanghai   Taipei   Toronto

With offices in

Argentina   Austria   Brazil   Chile   Czech Republic   France   Greece
Guatemala   Hungary   Italy   Japan   Poland   Portugal   Singapore
South Korea   Switzerland   Thailand   Turkey   Ukraine   Vietnam

OXFORD AND OXFORD ENGLISH ARE REGISTERED TRADEMARKS OF
Oxford University Press in certain countries.

© Oxford University Press 2009

Database right Oxford University Press (maker)

Editorial Director: Laura Pearson
Publishing Manager: Erik Gundersen
Managing Editor: Louisa van Houten
Development Editor: Tracey Gibbins
Design Director: Susan Sanguily
Design Manager: Maj-Britt Hagsted
Senior Designer: Michael Steinhofer
Production Artist: Elissa Santos
Image Editor: Robin Fadool
Design Production Manager: Stephen White
Manufacturing Coordinator: Eve Wong
Production Coordinator: Elizabeth Matsumoto

ISBN: 978 019 472786 0

Printed in China

10 9 8 7 6 5 4 3 2

Commissioned Illustrations by: Jonathan Burton pp. 40, 61; Gill Button pp. 14,
48, 54, 68; Leo Hartas p. 53; Belle Mellor pp. 20, 26, 46 76; Dettmer Otto
pp. 4; Roger Penwill pp. 31, 32, 72, 73; Gavin Reece pp. 12, 25, 81.

*The publishers would like to thank the following for permission to reproduce
photographs:* Alamy Images pp. 7 (Polish food store/Mark Sykes), 21 (wet
holiday/fstop2), 27 (teenage brother & sister/Digital Vision), 35 (low flying
aircraft/Arclight), 43 (Angelina Jolie/Allstar Picture Library), 43 (Vincent van
Gogh, self portrait/Lee Foster), 69 (umbrella/D. Hurst), 69 (glasses/Lenscap),
69 (bag/Ian Nolan), 75 (dog/Marvin Dembinsky Photo Associates), 77 (woman
with cat/Maria Galan Cats); Getty Images pp. 8 (painter/Marc Romanelli/
The Image Bank), 17 (dog/GK Hart/Vikki Hart/Stone), 23 (Statue of Liberty/
Stone/Getty Images/Daryl Benson; 25 (Stonehenge/Hugh Sitton/Stone), 24
(schoolboy/Brad Wilson/Stone), 30 (farmer/Mark Dadswell/AsiaPac), 30 (salt
flats/Theo Allofs/Photonica), 36 (architect/David Hanover/Stone), 43 (Justin
Timberlake/Getty Images/Bryan Bedder; 43 (Jane Austen/Hulton Archive), 43
(Marilyn Monroe/Gene Kornman/John Kobal Foundation/Hulton Archive), 43
(David Hockney/Gemma Levine/Hulton Archive), 50 (giraffes/Daryl Balfour/
Stone), 50 (lion cub/Brian Miller/Ovoworks/Time Life Pictures), 51 (safari
tourists/Randy Olson/National Geographic), 55 (stunt in action/Stone/Getty
Images/David Madison); 55 (stunt woman/Thinkstock/Jupiter Images/Getty
Images); 59 (dropped wallet/Taxi), 59 (test/Yellow Dog Productions/The Image
Bank), 65 (Albert Einstein/AFP), 82 (couple arguing/Altrendo Images); Jeremy
Sutton-Hibbert p. 11 (coffee cart girl); John Birdsall Social Issues Photo
Library pp. 39 (boy/John Birdsall), 80 (older man and carer/John Birdsall);
KOR Communications Ltd p. 30 (Mandy Williams/Guy Newman); One
Laptop Per Child p. 64 (Fuseproject); OUP pp. 2 (girl/Photodisc), 2 (student/
Photodisc), 5 (friends in cafe/Phil James), 24 (woman/Digital Vision), 24
(mature man/Digital Vision), 38 (teenage girl/Photodisc), 60 (family/Digital
Vision), 69 (mobile phone/D. Hurst), 69 (coat/Paul Bricknell); Photolibrary
p. 15 (bread and butter pudding/Chris Bayley); PunchStock pp. 2 (businessman/
Stockbyte), 17 (man/Digital Vision), 17 (briefcase/Digital Vision), 19 (man
on train/Rubberball), 19 (smiling woman/PhotoAlto), 33 (home office/
Digital Vision), 45 (crowd/Glowimages), 57 (friends secrets/Digital Vision),
60 (mature friends/Digital Vision), 70 (woman behind desk/Digital Vision),
78 (interview/Image Source); Rex Features pp. 43 (JK Rowling/David Fisher),
43 (Bob Marley/Everett Collection), 43 (Robbie Williams/Matt Baron/BEI),
44 (David Hockney/Nils Jorgensen); Robert Harding Picture Library p. 8-9
(deserted croft/Lee Frost); Still Pictures p. 39 (Provence cottage/Biosphoto/
Giraud Philippe); The David Hockney No.1 U.S Trust p. 44 (David Hockney
A Bigger Splash, 1967, Acrylic on Canvas, 96x96" © DAVID HOCKNEY);
Travelodge p. 47 (Mr & Mrs Davidson/South West News Service). P2 (Japanese
man/Masterfile); pp. 2 (NY skyline/Bilderbox/Age Fotostock/Art Life Images/
Superstock); 34 (Family/Image Source/Art Life Images/Superstock; Alamy:
Gary Corbett p. 8–9 (farmhouse).

Spotlight on Testing: pp. 3, 11, 19 (Hispanic female/Fancy/Veer AGE Fotostock);
pp. 5, 13, 21 (Hispanic male/ StockByte/AGE Fotostock/George Doyle); pp. 7,
15, 23 (Asian female/ Tetra Images/ArtLifeImages/Superstock); pp. 9, 17, 25
(Caucasian male/ Westend61/ArtLifeImages/Superstock/Hanno Keppel).

ACKNOWLEDGEMENTS

*The authors and publisher are grateful to those who have given permission to reproduce
the following extracts and adaptations of copyright material:* p. 13 'How trolley
girl read the market to become queen of fast by the times', The Times,
25/08/2007. © NI Syndication 2007 p. 49 'The couple who stopped at a
Travelodge and stayed for 22 years' by Paul Sims, Daily Mail, 11/09/02007.
© Daily Mail 2007.

*Although every effort has been made to trace and contact copyright holders before
publication, this has not been possible in some cases. We apologize for any apparent
infringement of copyright and if notified, the publisher will be pleased to rectify any
errors or omissions at the earliest opportunity.*